YOU DON'T LOOK FAT, YOU LOOK CRAZY

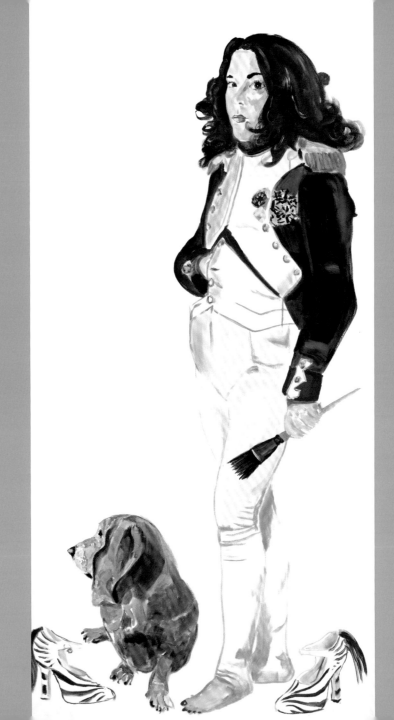

YOU DON'T LOOK FAT, YOU LOOK CRAZY

Ashley Longshore

Regan Arts.

Regan Arts.

65 Bleecker Street
New York, NY 10012

First Regan Arts edition,
February 2017

Library of Congress Control
Number: 2016939713

ISBN 978-1-68245-044-4

Names and identifying details of
some of the people portrayed in
this book have been changed.

Interior design by Alisha Petro

Cover and interior art by
Ashley Longshore

Cover design by Richard Ljoenes

Printed in China

10 9 8 7 6 5 4 3 2

To my pappy, my family, the love of my life Michael, and to all of my collectors who believed in me along the way, and not only just believed in me, but spent their hard-earned money on my work. Every single one of you is a part of my story and the reason I am where I am now . . . and on that note, I'd like to thank all of the galleries who said I wasn't marketable and the mean girls who said I would never amount to anything . . . suck it bitches . . .

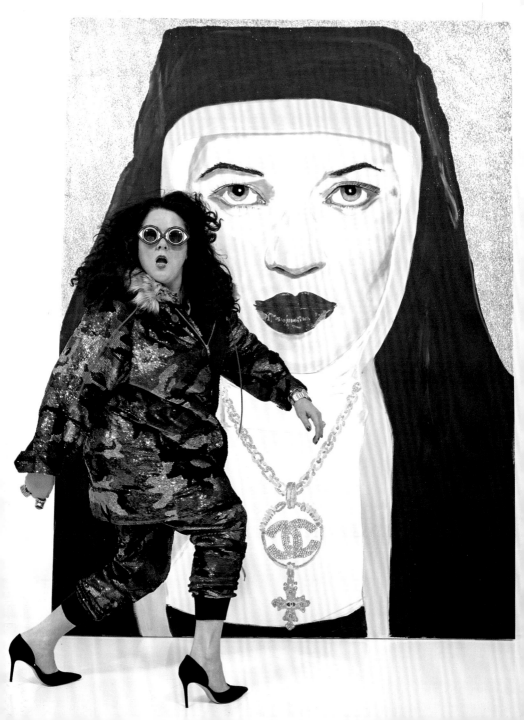

1

My Name Is Ashley Motherfucking Longshore

OKAY, Y'ALL listen, you. You bought this book—you *asked*—so here it goes.

My name is Ashley Motherfucking Longshore. I'm a self-taught artist, originally from Montgomery, Alabama. I'm an entrepreneur. I'm an American. I'm a woman. And I am really grateful to have been born in this wonderful motherfucking country.

Here's the thing, though. Growing up in the South, I was raised to be a trophy wife, to be the chair of one thing or another, to espouse meaningless causes, to be president of the Junior League or secretary of the Garden Club, or all of the above. I should be driving a Mercedes-Benz SUV full of screaming kids, rushing home to my lawyer husband, who won't be back till late because he's banging his trainer, but I didn't go that route. That's because I'm different. I was born different.

I was the weird kid who got picked on because I had a big voice and a loud personality, and I insisted on doing things my way. Or not at all.

Started early, too. All the way back in kindergarten. I had so much energy, my mother tried to exhaust me with extracurricular activities: ballet, tap, jazz, voice, gymnastics, swimming. Not painting, though. I was a ball of fire. Momma didn't think I could sit still long enough to paint.

That poor woman. Tried so hard to turn me into a Southern lady.

"Why have you got to be so *different*, child?" she'd say. "Why can't you be like these other *darling* girls?"

"I don't know," I'd say. "I'm sorry."

And I wept. Because being different is challenging.

I tried, though. Tried almost as hard as she did. I went to little-girl tea parties in the finest lace dresses. I went to kiddie balls. I wore a bonnet every Easter, for Christ's sake, and if I took it off, I didn't get to eat any of my yummy chocolate bunnies.

And speaking of dudes on the cross, don't get me started on Sunday school. *What are we doing indoors in this sweltering heat, belting out sappy hymns and hollering hallelujahs? I mean, seriously, is this "God's way"?*

As I got older, I tried to rein in my energy, but it wasn't easy. I hated those starchy dresses and pinchy shoes. I hated having my hair done. I hated standing up

"I DO DECLARE," MY MOTHER WOULD SAY, CLEARLY AT THE END OF HER ROPE. "I DON'T KNOW WHAT'S GOING TO BECOME OF YOU, SARAH ASHLEY."

HARVARD BUSINESS REVIEW

Having The Cake, Eating The Cake, Making The Cake Your Bitch

A guide to cake acquisition and distribution

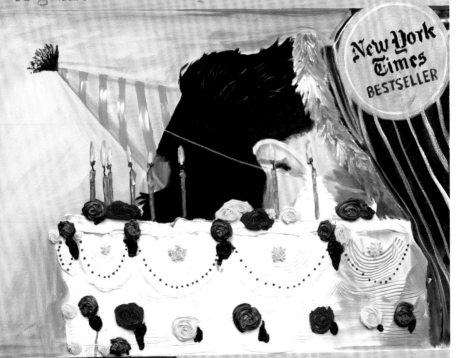

New York Times BESTSELLER

HARVARD UNIVERSITY PRESS

Ashley Longshore

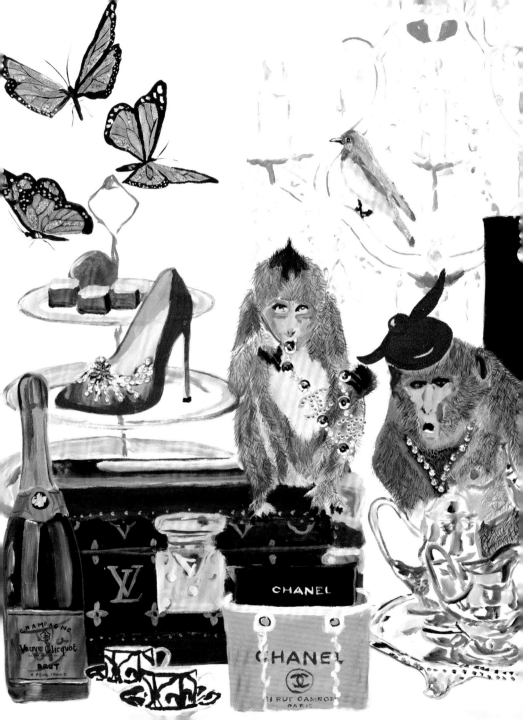

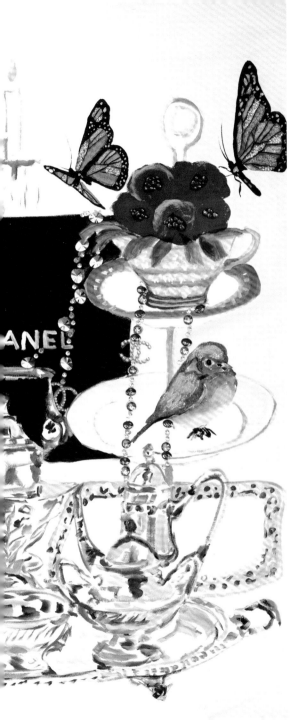

straight, like those future home-wreckers of America, and learning how to smile "from the inside."

"I do declare," my mother would say, clearly at the end of her rope. "I don't know what's going to become of you, Sarah Ashley."

That didn't bode well. It gave me a lot of angst about the future. By the time I was a pubescent teen, I was already wondering: *What is wrong with me? Why am I not thinking about the cotillion? And what's all this talk about those new folks across the street not having the right pedigree? I thought pedigrees were for dogs?*

Then one fine day, shortly after I turned sixteen, my parents went away for the weekend. I threw a wild party to celebrate. *Best party evah!* Except in the middle of the wild festivities, my mother walked

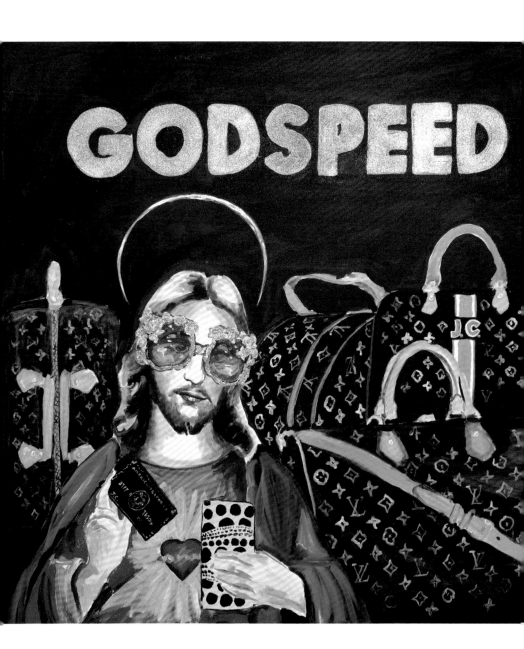

They celebrated my difference. They let me be whatever I wanted to be. And you know what I was? A straight-A student, that's what.

in unannounced and sent everyone home. She said she was psychic—had a feeling, turned that car right around, and sped the hell back.

Found my stash, too. Was about to flush it down the toilet when she thought better of it and called the cops instead. Narced me the hell out. Her own daughter. To the cops. Asked me to narc out my friends, but I refused, of course, because I'm a true lady.

"You are your father's child!" my mother said in that lilting wail, the back of her hand pressed to her moist forehead. "I can't do this a moment longer. You, young lady, are going to boarding school."

Oh, my God! Seriously? *Best thing evah.*

I ended up at Brenau Academy, the oldest girls' preparatory school in the sacred state of Georgia. And

guess what, bitches, they loved me. They loved my energy. They celebrated my *difference.* They let me be whatever I wanted to be. And you know what I was? A straight-A student, that's what. I got so many awards and commen-dations that people thought the system was rigged. I was voted "Class Favorite" and "Most Likely to Succeed."

Imagine that. Me. Miss Different.

Momma, I'm gonna tell you where you can put that Easter bonnet.

2
Painting Masturbating Couples in Montana

AFTER GRADUATING with honors, I went to Ole Miss, to make my parents happy. Ole Miss felt like a cuntry club. (And yes, I spelled that correctly.) Sorority rush, my God—what is that? Pi Beta Phi this, bitches. Girls squealing with delight when they got in, fainting in horror when they didn't. *The mission of our blessed sorority is to promote friendship among accomplished young women.* Excuse me for hurling.

I lasted six weeks. Went home. *Sorry, can't do it.*

My mother was devastated. She'd had my entire life planned out from the day I popped out of her vajayjay. I'm sure it would've been easier to dress pretty, fawn over those big-eared boys, and learn my dance steps, but I couldn't do it. Not even a choice, really. More like a voice in my head saying, *Ashley Longshore, you are never going to be like these other girls, so get used to it.*

True story: The day I left Ole Miss, some dude on the radio was singing some mournful song about Montana. I liked the sound of his voice and I liked the sound of Montana, so I got home and I told my daddy, "Daddy, I want to go to Montana." And he said, "Cool." And the next thing I know, our flight is landing in Missoula, and I could see the U of M campus from the air, nestled in there among the mountains. I looked at my daddy and said, "Wow, this is an adventure. This is what I want."

It got better. Trees and wide-open spaces and bowlegged men in hiking boots. And not a single Southern belle in sight.

"Looks nice," my father said.

I hugged him close. All I could think was, *Bless his advertising executive soul.*

Before I knew it, I was snow-boarding, hunting pheasants, and fly-fishing with flies I had tied myself. *From bird feathers.* They were real *purdy,* and the trout seemed to like them a lot more than everyone else's flies, maybe because I used my own pubic hair. The shit you do when you're stoned. Crazy.

Then one day I was in town and found myself looking in the window of a paint store. Not Benjamin Moore paint—I'm talking *paint* paint, for artists and tortured souls and such. My father had given me an American Express card to use in emergencies, and this wasn't exactly an emergency, so I called him long-distance, collect. "Daddy, I'm going to get a hobby," I said. "I want to paint and play drums."

And my daddy said, "Okay."

BEING AMBITCHOUS MEANS BEING A BIGGER BITCH THAN THE AVERAGE BITCH.

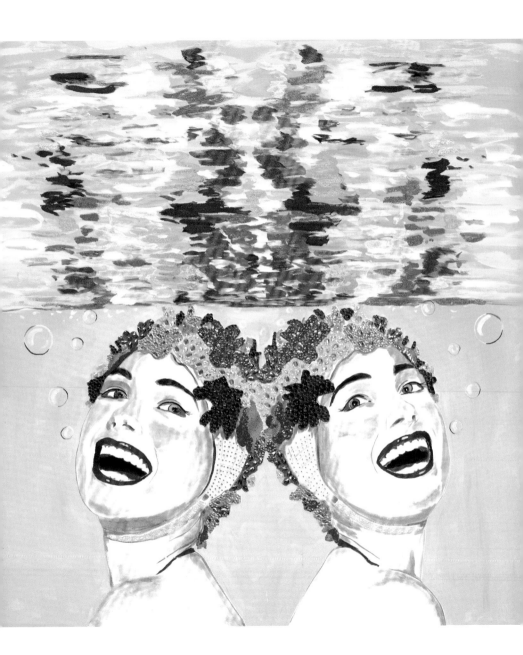

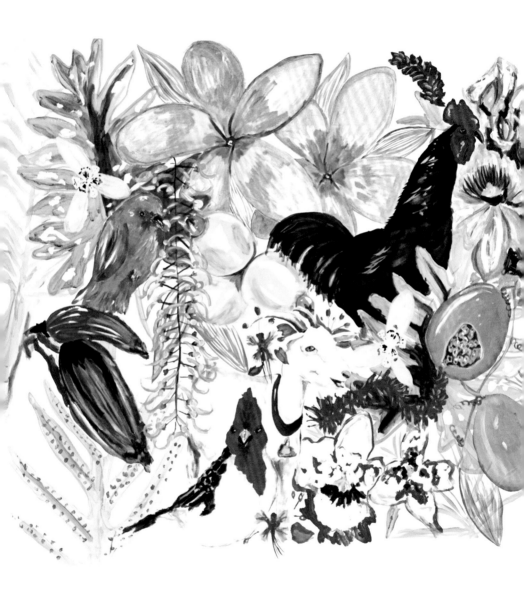

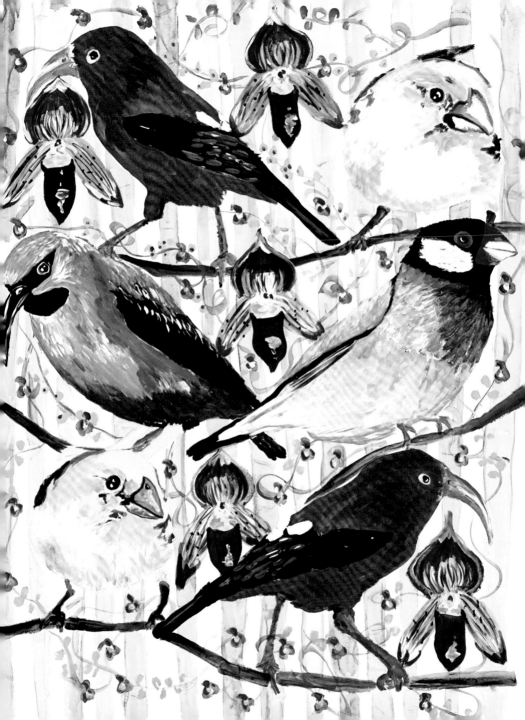

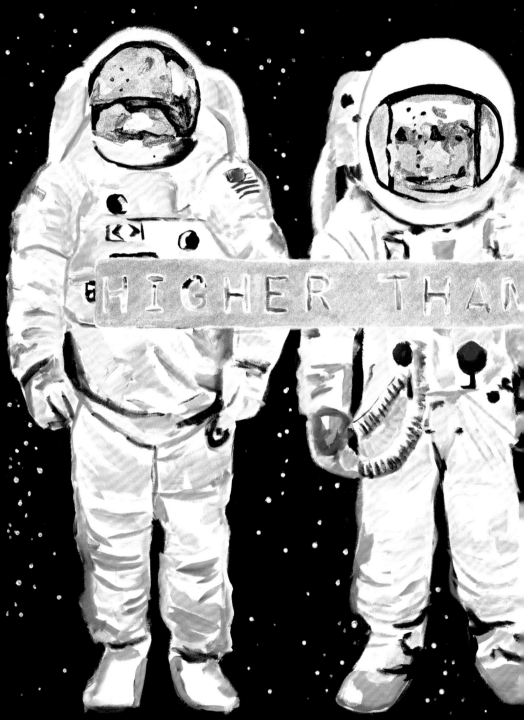

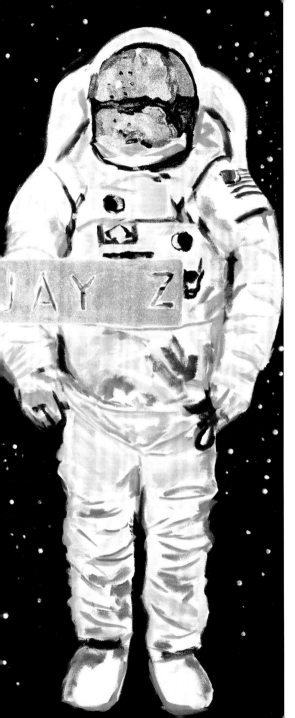

I bought forty-seven dollars' worth of brushes, canvases, and paint, went across the street and bought a pair of Pearl bongo drums, and went back to my dorm and started painting. Ten minutes later, I looked up at the clock and it was like, "Holy shit! Seven hours have gone by."

I took a break, and for the next hour or two, I wailed away on those bongos. But the painting took precedence. I couldn't stop.

My first finished painting was of a dancing bear. Don't ask me why. I painted some nature shit, too, because it was all around me. I'm telling you, in Montana there is no getting away from nature.

Then I painted a masturbating couple. They looked whimsical and kind of foreign, like they lived in Rio de Janeiro or some-thing, and I put them on separate canvases so they could masturbate privately. Then I painted a French couple, also masturbating. I can't for the life of me figure out why masturbating was so important to me. Can you? (But if I die before my time, I'd like my little sister to hurry over and empty out my nightstand drawer. Lord, there's enough dildos and lube to raise the *Titanic* in that thing—and any woman who's honest will tell you the same thing.)

After I'd done half a dozen paintings, I borrowed a camera and took photographs of my work. I was a complete beginner, but I decided I should start getting my portfolio together right away. Why wait? I then found out that art galleries prefer slides to photographs, so I went back, made slides, and began submitting them around town. I got a succession of *fuck you* letters. "Thank you so much for submitting your work. We're currently not taking any new artists." Or, "Thank you for your interest in our wonderful gallery. We do not work in this genre." Or my favorite, "Good luck finding someone to market your shit," (but not in those exact words). Let me tell you, I've been turned down more fucking times than a bed in a cheap motel.

It was upsetting—*then*. But occasionally I think back to those early days and can't help but gloat. *Y'all didn't think my work was marketable? How do you fools feel now?*

That's today. Back then, though, I did a lot of sobbing. Sometimes I'd call my dad and sob a little for him. Bless that man. He was so kind. All he wanted was for my sister and me to be happy. He was a self-made entrepreneur, so he knew it was tough, especially for women, and even more for sensitive *Southern* women. And since he was a man, and couldn't help but think like a man, he sometimes talked like a man. "Don't worry your pretty little head, Ash. You and your sister are going to find yourselves some really nice guys that are gonna take care of y'all. Ashley, you'll be able to paint all the livelong day, and Allyson's going to be free to do her fashion thang, and you are both going to lead good, *happy* lives."

For about a minute, every time I spoke to my daddy, I'd let my imagination run wild. I'd picture myself in a fancy SUV with seven screaming kids, and I'd picture the rich husband, who, for some inexplicable reason, had bought me a strap-on for my birthday. (It's for your pleasure, honey, so you should have waited for *your* birthday.) I'd wake up smiling in a big house, have breakfast, and do my Kegels (because, ladies, you gotta keep it tight to stay right), and then go off to play tennis for an hour and have lunch with the girls. After lunch, I'd call the nanny and ask her to please pick up the kids from school because I'd had one drink too many. Then I'd go home and nap until my trainer shows up. My trainer is hot. I try not to think about that.

I'd also picture myself on a bed, naked, covered in hundred-dollar

BEING AMBITCHOUS
IS COMPLETELY RELATIVE
TO THE SUBJECT, BUT
I WAS ALWAYS TAUGHT
THAT IT'S IMPORTANT
TO BE AMBITCHOUS IN
ONE WAY OR ANOTHER.
IT'S WHAT DRIVES YOU,
WHAT LIGHTS THE FIRE
UNDER YOUR ASS AND
LETS YOU ACCOMPLISH
AMAZING THINGS.

THE ART OF

BEING

AMBITCHOUS

Ashley Longsho

#1
New York
Times
Bestseller

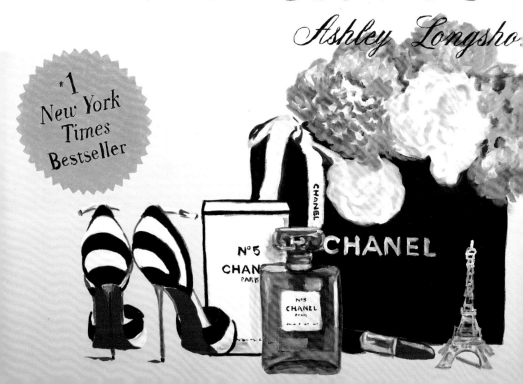

bills, next to a guy who's not my husband. Who could also be my trainer.

But then I'd get past those misleadingly seductive images and remember that I was a *woman,* goddamn it, and I wanted to make my own money—that I didn't need anyone to take care of me except myself.

Because even though my daddy wanted his girls to be taken care of, he also raised me to work hard, strive for success, and be *ambitchous* (well, he probably didn't use that word). Being ambitchous means being a bigger bitch than the average bitch. And being a "bitch" isn't about being mean to other women—it means smashing goals, excelling, and not fucking apologizing for it.

Your ambitchion could be sucking the biggest dick to get the biggest crocodile Birkin that has ever been made, or it could be fighting fiercely to make it in a male-dominated world. Being ambitchous is completely relative to the subject, but I was always taught that it's important to be ambitchous in one way or another. It's what drives you, what lights the fire under your ass and lets you accomplish amazing shit.

And honestly, I couldn't see myself walking up to my husband and asking for permission to buy a pair of Louboutin shoes. I mean, if you can tell teenagers that it means so much more *when they earn it themselves,* why can't you tell that to a grown-ass woman? I'd much rather wake up early, work hard, and rely on myself than fuck a guy who's long in the nut and have his testicles scraping over my nose three times a day just to get a new Chanel bag. That just isn't fucking worth it.

I had value, damn it. I knew that if I worked hard and painted like my life depended on it, people would eventually take notice. Until such time, however, I could cry. And I did. But then I'd dry my tears and watch it snow, or go float down a roaring river in a rubber raft, or learn to ride horses, or camp with buff guys with big-ass beards. Being surrounded

I'd also picture myself on a bed, naked, covered in hundred-dollar bills, next to a guy who's not my husband.

by nature showed me that there was more to life than status and greed. It was awesome. I was out duck hunting one morning with a Remington side-by-side, and dawn broke, and ten thousand geese flew across the rosy morning sky. Holy shit, God can paint!

One day I called my dad. "I'm taking a semester off," I said. "I need a break from finite math, the humanities, and literature. And frankly, I don't know why the hell I'm taking literature, because I hate to read."

"That's not going to happen, Ash," my father said. "You are staying in school."

I didn't argue with him. There was no point. I'd already dropped all my classes. I didn't have time for academics. I was busy painting. I took more photographs of my work and decided to visit the local galleries in person. I mean, *I am Ashley Motherfucking Longshore! How could these people resist?*

And here's the thing: Looking at the galleries in Missoula, I saw a lot of paintings of elk, bald eagles, and Native Americans astride handsome steeds. What I didn't see was masturbating foreigners. Then I walked into the very last place on my list, and I was delighted to find that they *weren't* fans of nature, or even the Old West. They actually had some stuff on the walls that was open to interpretation.

The owner wasn't there, unfortunately, so I left my portfolio with her assistant. And the very next day, the owner called and asked me to come in for coffee. "You're not bad," she said. "I'll give you a show."

I wanted to hug her. She was this really nice lady, and I found out later that she was the daughter of a foreign former president. She ended up buying my masturbating French couple and putting the painting on the most prominent wall in her dining room. She thought it made a great conversation piece. "How many times a day do y'all masturbate?" she'd ask her dinner guests, in that sexy accent.

I INVITED everyone I knew to the opening night, and asked them to invite everyone they knew. I walked around campus handing out flyers to complete strangers, talking in that loud "big girl" voice that used to get on my mother's nerves. "Hey, ya'll! Big art opening in Missoula tonight. Should be loads of fun."

Then I had this crazy idea that I wanted the show to be like an art opening in Prague. I'd never been to Prague, but I knew they were partial to loud techno music,

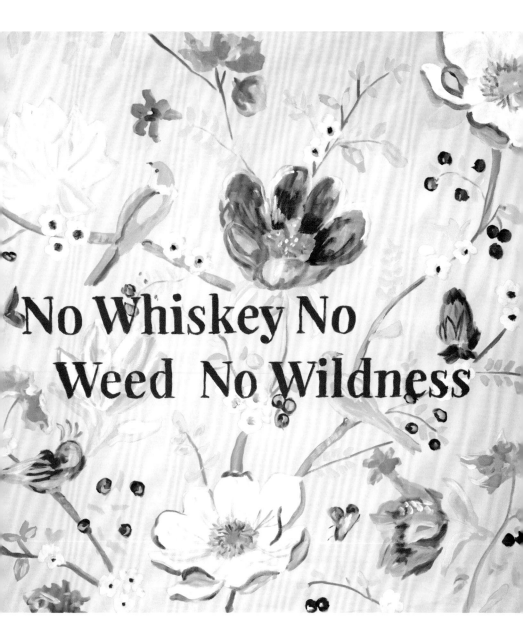

No Whiskey No Weed No Wildness

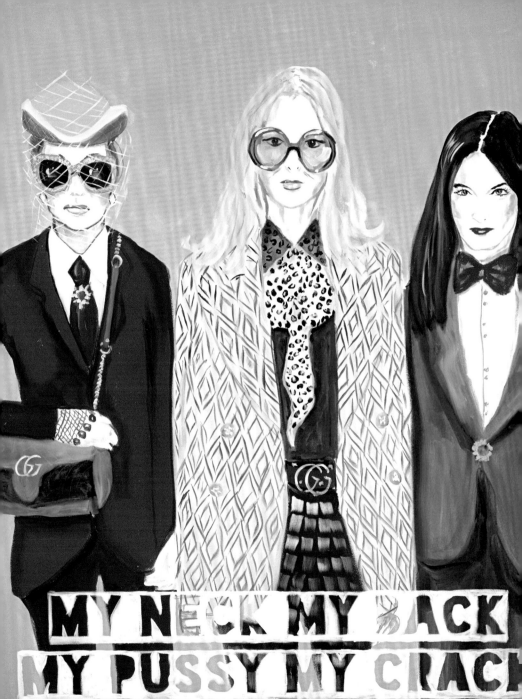

MY NECK MY BACK
MY PUSSY MY CRACK

and I'd read that they were also big on "performance" art. So I asked my friend Sally to come and pose in front of the guests during the festivities, right there in the gallery, so I could paint her live, and people could watch a real artist at work.

Then I called the local paper and told them that they shouldn't miss the show. It was going to be the best opening this side of Czechoslovakia. (Only I couldn't spell Czechoslovakia, so I said Prague.) "You guys really need to be there," I said. "This is not something you want to miss."

The show was a big hit, and my friends had a wonderful time, mostly because we all smoked a shit-ton of weed before we went. But even my nonfriends seemed to enjoy it, too. And the guy from the local paper was pretty impressed. He watched me paint my friend Sally, and made notes to himself in his little reporter's pad. The next day, the paper said nice things about my unusual work and described me as "gregarious."

I sold three paintings, for a total of $800. The gallerist got half. But then she used part of that to buy the French masturbators, so it all worked out.

I had arrived! I was an artist! People were paying actual money for an Ashley Longshore! I was going to make so much money that I wasn't going to be able to spend it!

The next day I went to the local farmers' market and bought a massive basket of peaches. Then I went to a local store and found a greeting card of a man in leather chaps and nothing else, with his hairy ass front and center. I wrote the reporter a note. "Thank you so much for the fucking exposure. I really appreciate it. Love, Ashley Longshore."

I delivered the peaches and the card in person, and the next day, they mentioned it in the editorial. It was accompanied by an image of the card, and they included my note, but edited out the word "fucking."

I was cool with that.

The next day, I sold another painting. I was rich!

Well, not rich. But it was my first show, and I'd sold several pieces. Ask me if that was addictive.

3

The Boyfriend
from Moneyville,
USA

OKAY, I'VE left out an important part of the story. The Boyfriend. I had been seeing The Boyfriend for a couple of years, and he was kind of a dick, but part of me—the insecure part—believed I liked him. His family had a big spread on the East Coast, as well as houses everywhere else in the fucking world.

The Boyfriend was trying to take a stab at normalcy, though, or maybe just trying to piss off his wealthy family, so he'd been working as a chef. I guess he was pretty good at that, but in real life, he was dour and miserable, and later I realized that it ran in the family. It was kind of fascinating. These people were making more interest on their money in a day than they could spend in a year; they had money pouring out of every orifice, and they were all incredibly unhappy. And sure, I know, it's a cliché. *Money doesn't make you happy.* But having a little money sure helps, pal, and for these people, it didn't seem to be helping them at all.

And, look, as long as we're being honest, my family wasn't exactly poor. I had a father who paid for my education. Bought me shit. Had my back. I was lucky. But my father was a nice guy, and a self-made man, and these people were assholes. I wondered whether it was *cultural*. I was a genteel girl from the Deep South, and these people were East Coast money—the kind of big-toothed people who reminded you at every turn that their people had come over on the *Mayflower.*

Good lesson, though. Teachable moment. And I made a mental note to myself: *Money is not the answer.*

I've got to say, though, from where I was standing, I don't think any of those people would have agreed with me. For them, it seemed to be *all* about money. "Oh, you got the *small* Birkin. I got the big one." Or, "Oh, my God, Muffy, you've been dieting! You look good. Another twenty, thirty pounds, and you're *there.*"

It was astonishing. That level of bitchiness. Didn't these people have anything better to do? Oops. I guess they knew the answer to that: They didn't. This was a sport to them, and a very competitive sport at that.

I remember thinking, *Ashley, girl, you are never going to get caught up in that shit.*

On the other hand, as an artist with an eye for the finer things in life, I had to admit that those Birkin bags were awfully pretty.

But no! I told myself I couldn't think like that. I knew where that would lead. Before long, I'd be a total show pony, with a convertible Bentley, a waterfront spread in the Hamptons, and a diamond so big my whole body would be listing to the left. *Hey . . . that doesn't sound half bad!*

No! Stop! Pull yourself together, Ash. Not going to happen.

"Oh, honey, those shoes are so last season."

AS AN ARTIST WITH AN EYE FOR THE FINER THINGS IN LIFE, I HAD TO ADMIT THAT THOSE BIRKIN BAGS WERE AWFULLY PRETTY.

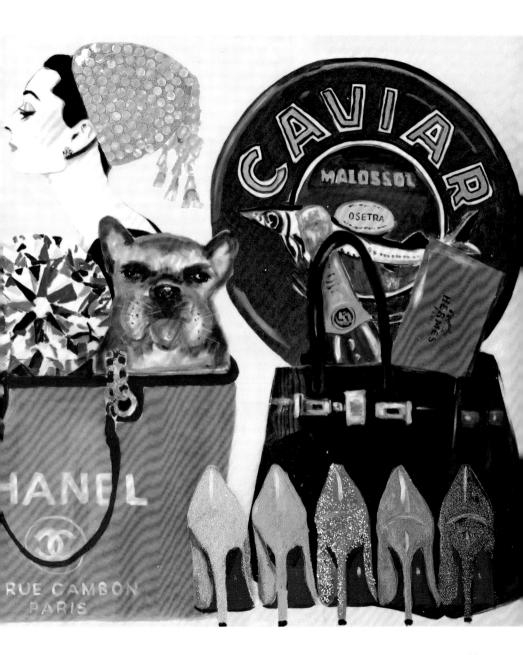

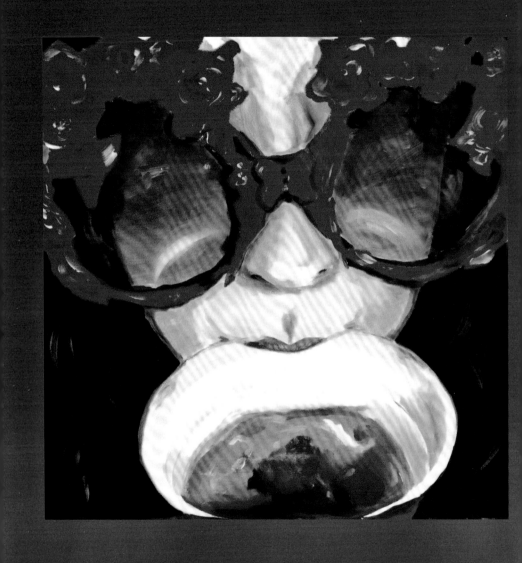

YOU'VE GOT TO LEARN TO DEPEND ON YOURSELF, EVEN IF IT'S HARD, AND MAYBE ESPECIALLY WHEN IT'S HARD.

Shoes? I'm wearing Gore-Tex hiking boots I got from Hippies "R" Us in Missoula. I'm not going to get sucked into your whole peacocking shit. *Ashley, don't play that game.* (Although, then again, I must say—and I'm only talking aesthetically here—Mr. Louboutin does make a very nice shoe.)

ANYWAY, after college, The Boyfriend and I moved to the East Coast. He got work as a chef and I painted. I did what I'd done in Montana, making the rounds of local galleries, and I got a lot of *fuck yous* before a sophisticated gentleman with great taste decided to represent me. I made a thousand dollars one month, two thousand the next, and it should have been more—except somewhere out there in *The Big Book of How to Take Advantage of Artists* some asshole had decided that the galleries were entitled to 50 percent.

On bad months, I'd hit my daddy up for a so-called loan, but he wanted me to try to figure it out for myself. "I know you're trying, honey, and I would never tell you to maybe look in the classifieds for a job, but it's a thought."

Come on! I'm an artist.

So I was stuck with The Boyfriend, and it began to look like this yin and yang business is definitely true. He was an asshole, but he paid the rent—or, technically, his parents paid the rent—and that was good for me. (Is that the yin or the yang?) Unfortunately, he was also an asshole about that. "I pay the rent, Ashley! Let's try not to forget that."

I'd think, *What exactly does that mean—that you expect me to take out the garbage every night?* Well, yeah. Sort of. Kind of. Because that's how it works, right? That's how everything works. That's how *life* works. There's no free lunch, yada, yada, yada.

And you know what? I didn't want it to work like that for me. I didn't want this asshole paying my rent. Well, okay, a few more months weren't going to hurt, right? We've all got to deal with a *little* humiliation, but if I kept painting like a whirling dervish, I knew I'd land on my own two feet.

Jesus! The excuses we make; the lies we tell ourselves. I was weak. I kept putting up with that asshole. And he wasn't just an asshole about the rent, either. He was an asshole with other people. Every time we went out to dinner, for example, he'd send his plate back. "This is overcooked," or, "I could get a better béarnaise sauce from a jar," or, "Is the chef off tonight?"

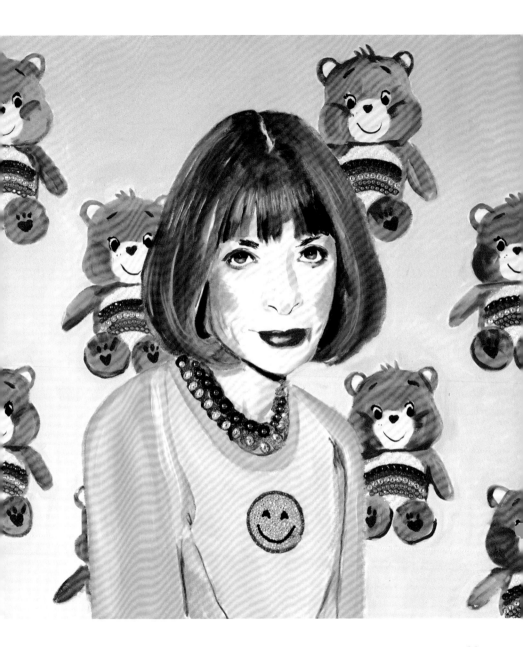

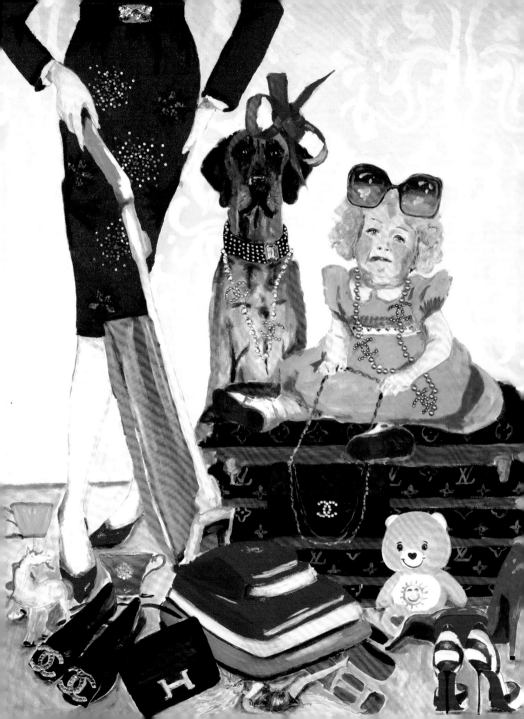

Then one day, The Boyfriend and I were lounging around, and he decided to make chocolate chip cookies. I thought they were perfect, piping hot, with just the right amount of chew, but he didn't like them. He thought they weren't *crispy* enough. And just as I was reaching for another subpar chocolate chip cookie, he grabbed the tray, crossed to the back door, and pitched the entire batch into the yard.

I was like, "I'm done! This is crazy!" Suddenly, I didn't care that he paid the rent. I didn't care about his trust fund, and I certainly didn't care that he'd probably buy me a convertible Bentley once we got married. So, I walked out, rented a U-Haul, packed my shit, and drove all the way from Moneyville, USA, to Charleston, South Carolina, to crash with my little sister, who was going to college there. Nine hundred and forty-two point four miles, and I did the drive in one day. I left at six in the morning and got there just before midnight.

I was a little upset with my sister—she didn't have any chilled wine or hors d'oeuvres waiting for me, like those *comme il faut* East Coast assholes—but I was still in a talkative mood. My sister was young, impressionable. I had some

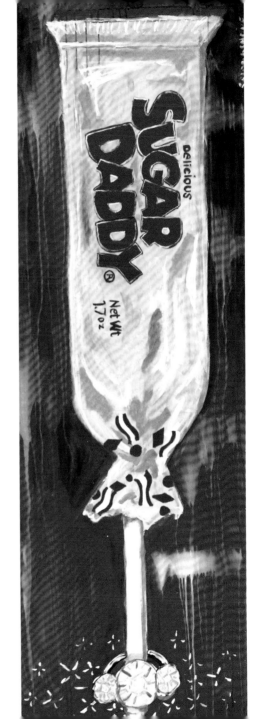

older-sister shit to impart. "This boyfriend business isn't what it's cracked up to be," I told her. "It's a fantasy, Allyson. You've got to learn to depend on yourself, even if it's hard, and maybe especially when it's hard."

After spending two nights with Allyson, I drove out to see my dad at his beach house in the Redneck Riviera. He was very happy to see me. In fact, he was relieved. He had never liked The Boyfriend. He knew he was an asshole, and he knew he wasn't making me happy.

I knew better than to ask him for money—he had been good enough to pay for college, and smart enough to cut me off right after I graduated—but he let me set up a little art studio in his garage. I painted every day, all day, and at the end of the day, I celebrated by smoking a little doobie. I also knew I needed to start making a living, so I asked my father to let me know if he heard of anything. "But I'm still going to be an artist," I said.

And he said, "Lord, child, the only thing harder than being an artist is being a poet." And I said, "I don't care. It's what I want. And I know I can do it." I was also thankful I don't like poetry. Except for Andrew Dice Clay, *There once was a man from Nantucket / Whose dick was so long he could suck it.* Or my other favorite, *Little Boy Blew / Hey! He needed the money.*

My father is in advertising, and at the time, he was working with a publishing group that was about to launch a magazine in New Orleans. He reached out to a colleague there, and I went up, interviewed, and got a job, and the following week, I packed another U-Haul and moved into a tiny apartment in a former New Orleans whorehouse, right in the heart of the Central Business District. The following Monday, I went to work at the magazine. I was twenty-eight years old. I was alone. But I was *happy.* I knew I was going to be okay. I had my shit together. I had good energy. I was a woman, not a young, insecure girl. Nobody was going to fuck with me.

And you want to hear something really strange? When I was in kindergarten, the teacher made each student pick two state flags from a coloring book and fill them out in the appropriate state colors. You want to know which states I chose? Montana and Louisiana. True story. Cue eerie music.

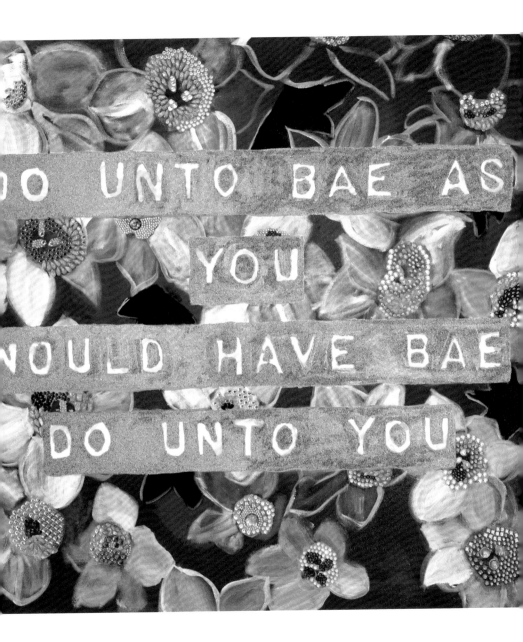

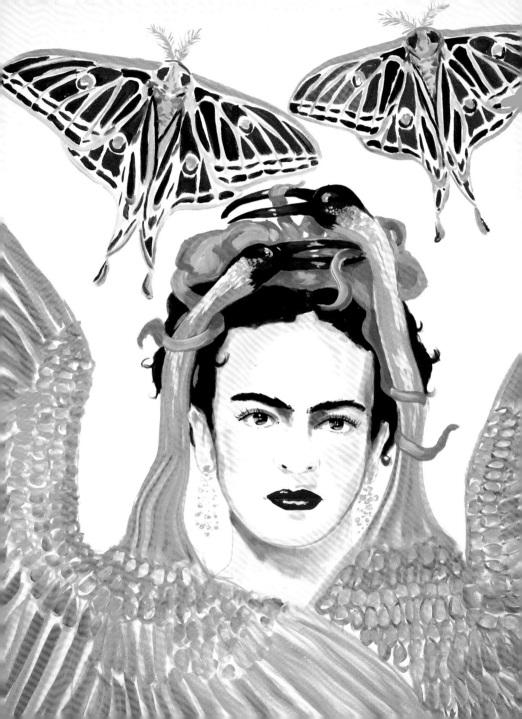

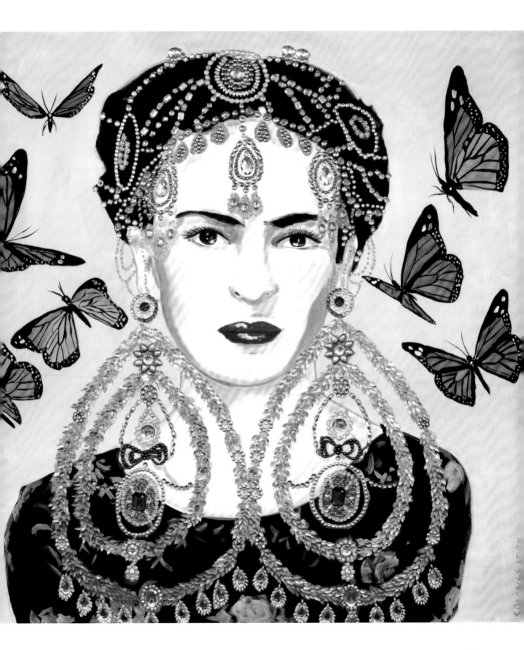

<u>4</u>
Getting Fired Can Light a Fire

I LOVED NEW ORLEANS.
My parents had actually taken
me there for my thirteenth
birthday. They had walked me
down Bourbon Street in the
afternoon, because it was more
age-appropriate at that hour, but
there were still people out in the
middle of the street, drinking beer
and stumbling around, and there
was loud music spilling out of the
bars, and plenty of women who
didn't look like they were wearing
undies. We were a long way from
Montgomery, and I liked it.

For the first six or seven months
living in New Orleans, I sold
magazine advertising. I was good
at it, too. I sold a shitload of ads.
I would come strolling back to the
office in my high heels, waving the
signed contracts in the air, and my
colleagues would hoot and holler,
congratulating me. But it felt a
little soulless. And I was neglect-
ing my art. I still painted, back at

the whorehouse, but there weren't enough hours in the day. But I did have some stuff to sell, so I made the rounds again, and this cool little art gallery on Julia Street agreed to represent me. (Sometimes you get lucky in life and actually meet people with taste.)

I couldn't get enough of the city. The people were kind of wild and bohemian, but at the same time had proper southern manners, a charming combination. They were approachable, curious, interested. And whenever anyone found out I was an artist (with a secret life selling advertising), many of them expressed immediate interest. Since I was both needy and shameless, I always pounced: "Would you like to see some of my work? I'd be glad to bring it over. At your convenience, of course."

More often than not, people said yes, and I'd reach for a pad and paper and ask them what their schedule looked like. And we'd work it out, *Tuesday at 4, after yoga,* and a few days later I'd pack several dozen paintings into the back of my big-ass Ford Expedition and drive over to the yogi's house.

It was crazy. People started buying my paintings. And whenever I'd travel—to visit friends in Atlanta and Minneapolis or to see my sister—I'd always take my portfolio along, and I'd cold-call galleries and head over with photographs of my work. I oozed charm. I talked loud and laughed loud. I was Miss Charisma.

I honestly don't know where I got the balls to do that, but I really wanted it, and I knew nobody was going to do it for me.

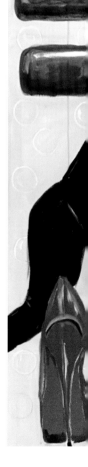

WE LIVE IN AMERICA. THIS ISN'T LIKE THE REST OF THE WORLD. A WOMAN CAN BE ANYTHING SHE WANTS IN THIS COUNTRY. YOU DON'T HAVE TO LIVE LIKE THIS.

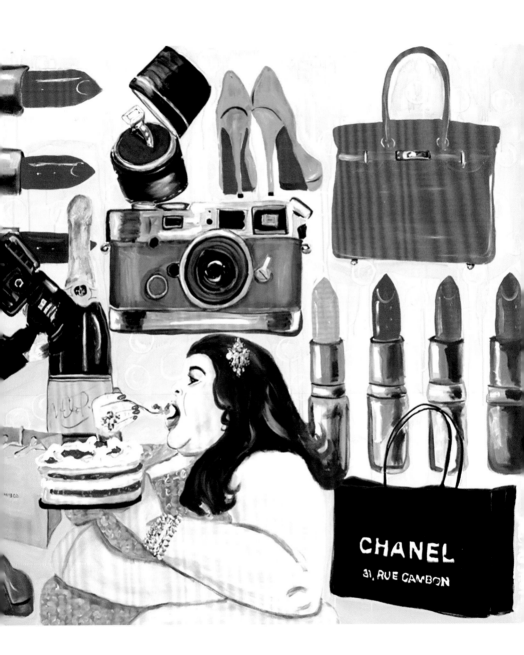

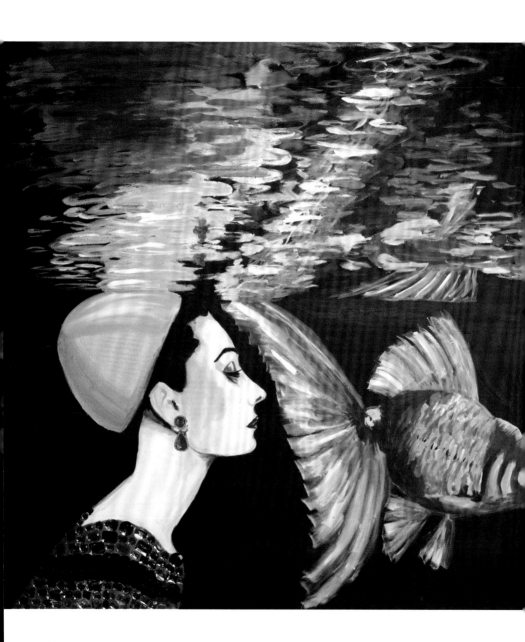

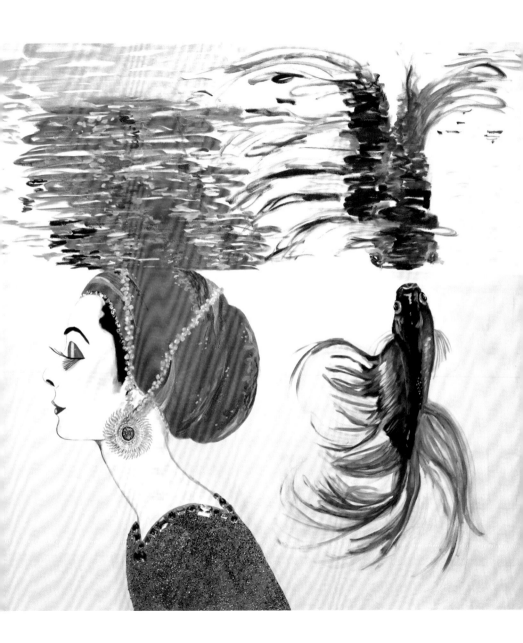

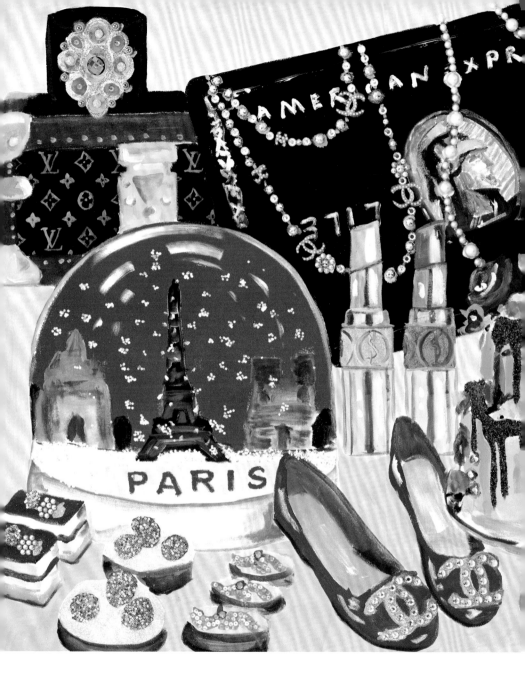

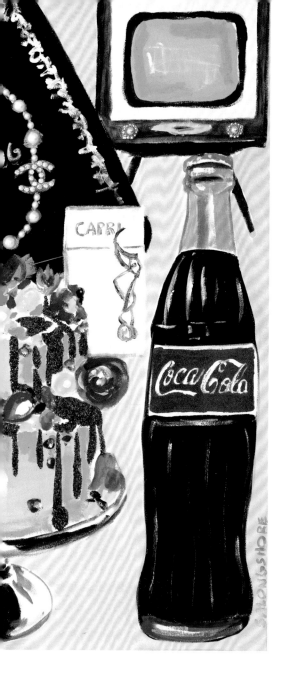

As Audrey Hepburn once said, "When you want a helping hand, look at the end of your arm."

I ended up selling a bunch of pieces long-distance. My plan was working. Well, starting to work. I wanted to conquer the world, but I had to start somewhere.

Some of my local clients insisted on meeting me, and many of them turned out to be exactly the type of woman I was raised to be. They'd be rushing off to lunch at the club or to Pilates class, or they'd take a call on their cell and go on about their kid's freshman year at Harvard, and they always had these big, happy smiles. But when they turned around and thought no one was looking, they seemed to be close to tears.

I used to think that could be me. I felt sorry for them, because they were completely reliant on their husbands for money—these women literally had to suck dick for anything they wanted. But it also confused me. I couldn't understand why they would choose a life that was so unfulfilling, when this great country of ours gives women the opportunity to do so much more than having the world's best ass. I wanted to grab them by their Givenchy lapels and shake some sense into their coiffed heads. We live in America. This isn't like the rest of the world. *A woman can be anything she wants in this country. You don't have to live like this.*

I mean if they wanted to, *fine.* But most of them seemed to be living on the edge of despair.

THESE WOMEN were not all that different from the women in that fancy East Coast Town That Must Not Be Named; they weren't much different from my own mother and the women in her social circle; but that had been a generation ago, and these women were my age—they were young. Young and miserable. Not all of them, of course, but lots of them— maybe even most of them.

It upset and aggravated me at the same time. But then I realized I was being judgmental. So I kept my mouth shut and instead used it in my art. Exhibit #1: She Sucked a Lot of Dick to Get That Louis Vuitton.

True story: I was shopping in L.A. and found this gorgeous purse for like seven or eight thousand dollars. It was a lot of purse, part of a pop collection, but it was too late: I was already in love. I looked at the salesgirl and said, "Wow, even I would suck dick for this purse." She started laughing. "Actually, I do get a lot of women who come in here, check out the purses, then disappear and return an hour later with a guy with a credit card. And honestly, their lips always look a little chafed."

Who was I to tell them how to live their lives? Who was I to say they were wrong? Nobody. It might not be how I do things, but, girl, if you want, you can go get yours.

MEANWHILE, I kept selling ads, until one day the entire operation was sold to another publisher. The new owners put me to work on a glossy design magazine, which was cool, because it felt closer to art. But then they moved me to another magazine, which was mostly real estate, and I thought that was beneath me, not cool, and I wasn't happy.

I had been telling myself that someday soon I would be able to support myself as an artist, only then, fueled by desperation, I told myself the same thing *in a much*

A CUBICLE! THAT'S LIKE PUTTING A LIONESS IN A CAGE. I PROMISED MYSELF I WOULD NEVER AGAIN WORK ANYWHERE WITH FUCKING CUBICLES.

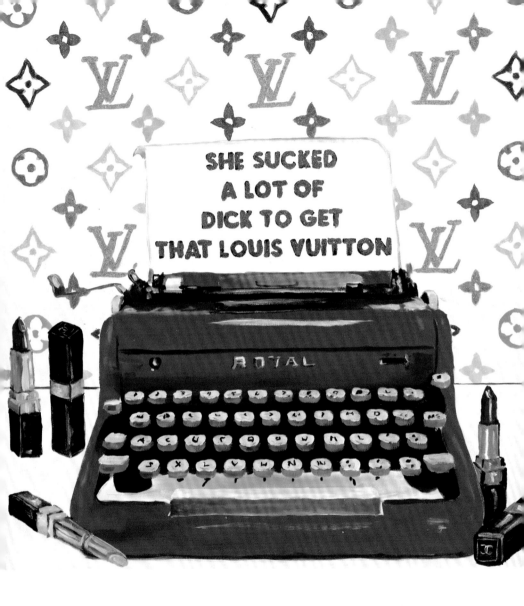

I looked at the salesgirl and said, "Wow, even I would suck dick for this purse."

louder voice. "You're going to be okay, Ashley. You *want* this. You work hard. You are going to prove yourself."

About a week into this fresh hell, I met a guy at Jazz Fest, and I crushed hard, and when he invited me to spend the weekend at his family's beach house, I couldn't resist. Sunday rolled around, and I wasn't in a rush to get back to New Orleans, so that Monday I called in sick. Was sick on Tuesday, too.

On Wednesday, I finally went back to work. I had a great tan, so I tried to balance it out by not wearing lip gloss, imagining that my pale, unadorned lips would give me a sickly, consumptive pallor. I got in the elevator and rode up to the sales floor, dreading the day ahead, then made my way along that Kafkaesque collection of open cubicles, en route to my own rabbit warren. I had never hated that office as much as I did at that very moment. A cubicle! That's like putting a lioness in a cage. I promised myself I would never again work anywhere with fucking cubicles.

My supervisor came over before I'd even lowered my buttocks into my chair. "Did you get that contract signed?" she asked. "From last week?" I'd had a bad week; I think I'd sold, like, one ad.

"God, you know, I didn't," I said. She went on her unhappy way. A few minutes later, the PA system blared to life: "Ashley Longshore, could you please report to Colleen's office?" Colleen was the ad director. I walked into her office, and she looked me up and down, admiring my tan and doubtless worrying about my pale, un-adorned lips. "How you feelin'?" she said. And I said, "You know, I'm actually feeling a little better." And she asked, "Did you get that contract signed?" I said, "No, I didn't." And she stuck her hand out, thanked me for my time, and fired me. *WTF? A girl can't go to the beach for a few days?* (Funnily enough, Colleen is now one of my favorite collectors, and she likes to take *full* credit for all of my artistic accomplishments— she really did light a fire under my ass by firing me.)

5
The Art of Self-Promotion

I DIDN'T SAY A WORD.
I went back to my cubicle, feeling a little fragile, then grabbed my things, got in the elevator, and went downstairs. I crossed the lobby, made my way through the parking lot, got into my Expedition, and immediately started sobbing. I'd just been fired. My father was going to kill me. It was a respectable job, and I'd been making almost $2,000 a month, enough to cover my rent and most of my expenses, but now—hell, I was probably going to get kicked out of the whorehouse.

I didn't want another job, though. I wanted to be an artist. So I went back to my apartment, parked myself in front of my computer and looked at my lovely website, sitting there, gathering dust. This was *Ashley Longshore's personal web page,* a long-ago gift from my wonderfully generous father, who, as an advertising man, understood the art of self-promotion. Ashley Longshore, *the artist.* I'd never taken advantage of the site, but I did then. I emailed everyone who had ever bought one of my paintings and everyone who had even thought about buying one of my paintings—and even everyone who didn't realize *I was a painter*—and I attached the link to my website. *Hey, look at me. It's Ashley. I'm a painter.* I had plenty of paintings available for sale, and I attached JPEGs of every last one.

God, there were tons. I was painting so prolifically that my studio was full of piles and piles of paintings—but as I always say: "If I don't paint it, I can't sell it." Maybe it would have been better to have had *nothing* for sale, to have been a limited-edition Birkin bag, for example, available only to the chosen few on The List,

thereby creating a frenzy of desire. Instead, my paintings were just sitting there, like sad puppies at the pound. Did I say $500? I'll take $50.

Okay, yes. We have our down moments, people. It happens. But I was going to make this work. *Attention must be paid, and all that.*

I sent out more emails. I emailed friends of friends. I tried to guess rich people's emails based on their rich-sounding names.

You have to understand, people. This was many years ago. This was before Snapchat, Instagram, and Twitter.

Meanwhile, I decided to paint as if my life depended on it. I wanted to believe that my entire *oeuvre* was going to sell in a matter of days, and that I needed to create inventory to meet the coming demand.

I wrote press releases to introduce myself to the media. I cold-called reporters, who either hung up on me or asked what I was wearing.

Still, I tried not to panic. I had less than a thousand dollars in my checking account, and I could still pay my rent. So what if I went a little hungry? Eating is overrated. (Not really, but sometimes you have to lie to yourself to get through the day.) Anyway, buying painting supplies was more important to me than buying food, and I believed

The name of the game is branding, people. It's about value. I'm trying to turn myself into a Birkin bag.

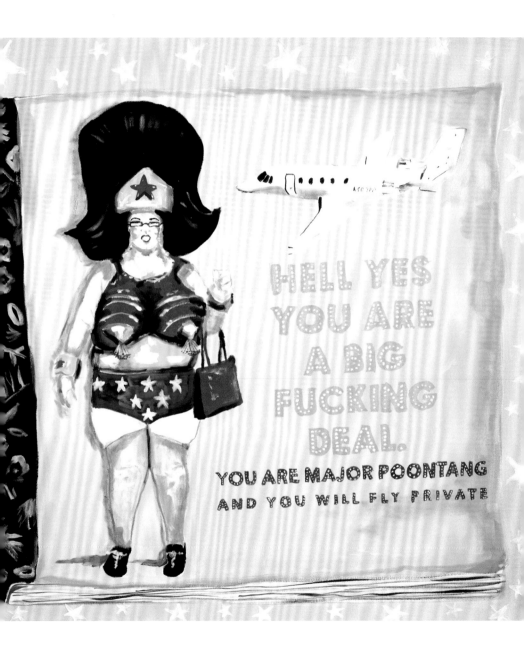

THERE'S A LESSON IN THERE SOMEWHERE . . . SOMETHING ABOUT NOBODY GIVING YOU NOTHING, SOMETHING ABOUT GETTING YOUR NAME OUT THERE, SOMETHING ABOUT MAKING SHIT HAPPEN FOR YOUR OWN SELF. OR AS MY DADDY LIKES TO SAY, "HE WHO TOOTS HIS OWN HORN CONTROLS THE VOLUME."

that making art was a better investment for my future than eating. I was like a racehorse with blinders on. Nothing was going to get in my way.

Then, miracle of miracles, slowly but surely, I began to sell paintings. Not many. Just a few here and there, enough to keep myself from slipping into total destitution. When a painting sold, I put a big SOLD sticker across the front. *Gone, bitches! You didn't move fast enough!* Every painting I sold lit a fire inside me. I was going to show everyone who ever said I couldn't do it that not only was I making art, but I was selling the shit out of it too. Whenever I left the house, I smiled and tried to look optimistic. And every time I was introduced to anyone, I told them I was an artist, that I'd love to show them my work, and that I would be happy to drive over to their house in my big-ass Expedition at their earliest convenience, like right that very minute, even. I did this without sounding desperate, though, delivering my lines with the aplomb of a Southern lady who didn't have a care in the world.

This was around 2004. I distinctly remember that because suddenly Facebook was the *next big thing,* and I immediately saw its potential: an opportunity to make new friends I didn't know! I reached out to all sorts of wonderful strangers, and we connected, and the next thing I knew, I'd be loading up the old truck and heading over. *No, no! No charge. I know other galleries charge $300 just to come over and look at your walls, but that's not the way Ashley rolls. Happy to be here. Let's see how it looks over the fireplace . . . Oh? You like it? Something for the house in Vail? Hmmm, let me think . . . possibly.*

Don't misunderstand. This didn't happen fast. But I did manage to eke out a living. I realized I wasn't getting enough exposure doing it alone, despite all my new collectors, so I went the gallery route. I wanted to see what more I could get from the art world. Two places actually offered to represent me, but I said no. This 50 percent shit didn't work for me. On the other hand, if they wanted to host a show, and they wanted to get reasonable about their rates, we could talk. Most galleries wouldn't budge. They still won't.

Again, I don't know where I got the balls to suggest this, all I know is that I wanted to succeed, on my own terms, and that I had to take some chances to make it happen. And it did begin to happen. I had a show, shared a doobie with friends, sold some stuff. Had another show, another doobie,

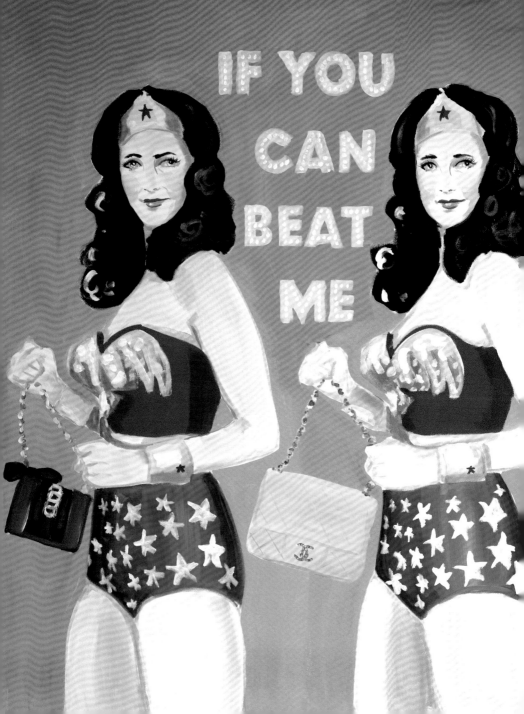

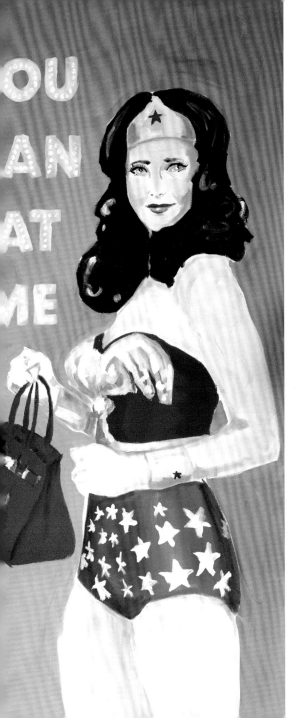

sold some more stuff. Not enough, mind you, but enough to make me believe that in the not-too-distant future I might actually be able to support myself as an artist.

It's all about self-promotion, people. A lot has changed since the Dark Ages of my late youth. There was no social media then. No tweeting. No Instagram. And YouTube didn't come along till much later. And, God, did I love YouTube! I started making little videos of myself and emailing them to everyone on my list. (Google "Ashley Longshore YouTube" and you'll get the general idea.) Compared to YouTube, email was Dullsville. With YouTube, I could be that loud, gregarious girl my mother had once considered medicating into quietude. YouTube was also *fun*. It didn't start that way—it started with desperation—but it became fun.

Today, with social media being what it is, I'm out there all day every day. And I'm not afraid to say whatever the fuck I want. (I say *fuck* a lot, I know; I'm sorry. It's my own personal exclamation point.) I like putting my personality out there; I like letting people get to know me, the artist behind the art. And if they find me offensive, well, they can get the fuck off my feed.

In the early days, when the press called, I put myself out there. I'd talk to anyone. Now, I'm a little more discerning about who I talk to, and who I talk about. ("Yes, it's true. I sell my work to movie stars and billionaires.") It's not just about me. Self-promotion is important for my fabulous and near-fabulous clients, and for that *totally fabulous* client who just wired $30,000 into my checking account. They want to see my name in print, too. They want to show the magazine to their friends. "This here is Ashley Longshore, that self-taught artist from Montgomery, Alabama, I've been telling you about. We have three of her pieces. We might commission an original."

The name of the game is *branding,* people. It's about value. I'm trying to turn myself into a Birkin bag.

And here's the thing: I sell to a lot of art collectors, which is great. It tells me they think I have value, that I'm an *investment.* But I also want people to buy my art because it speaks to them. The girl who puts aside 30 percent of her paycheck every month so

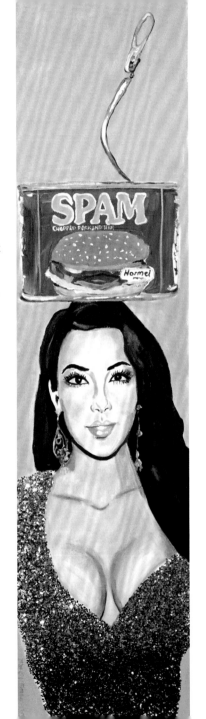

she can get the Chanel bag she's been dreaming about, that's who I want as a client, because that is who I am as a consumer. I'm not a billionaire or a movie star either! Someone who falls in love with one of my paintings and saves up their hard-earned cash because they absolutely have to have it? That's the kind of buyer who means the most to me.

IF ENOUGH PEOPLE fall in love with my work, I'll be a brand, and I'd like that good shit to happen *now,* while I'm still breathing. I mean, look at Van Gogh: Poor guy only ever sold one painting in his life. Didn't have Instagram. Born in the wrong century, I guess.

Of course, I'm not sure Van Gogh would have been a tireless self-promoter, and, as long as we're being honest here, that's what it takes.

Take the Kardashians. *Please.* I'm sure they serve an important role in society (not that I know what it is), and I love those fertility-god asses, but what impresses me most is their gift for branding. Nobody would know who these people were if Kim Kardashian hadn't put in that extra little wrist twist when she was making her home porno with Ray J (fuck yeah, I watched it. She looks damn good

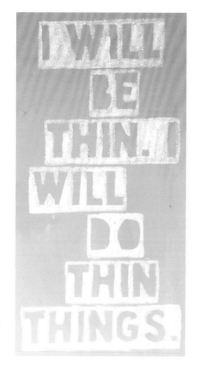

in it), but they've turned that into an empire. Those girls are closers. They can sell *nothing*—and that's exactly what they sell.

There's a lesson in there somewhere. Y'all figure it out. Something about nobody giving you nothing, something about getting your name out there, something about making shit happen for your own self. Or as my daddy likes to say, "He who toots his own horn controls the volume."

6

A Not-
So-Desperate
Housewife

I HAD ANOTHER LIFE, too—a life outside of my career. Remember that guy I met at Jazz Fest, the one whose parents had a house on the beach? Well, we were still tangling. And right around this time, my father decided to remarry, and Mr. Jazz Fest and I went to the wedding. I was very happy for my father. I loved my stepmother. I thought my daddy had done real good.

The wedding took place in Dallas, and there was a rehearsal dinner the night before. Mr. Jazz Fest and I got completely shit-faced. We spent most of the rest of the night driving around Dallas in a limousine, doing more drinking, smoking weed, and hitting the clubs until they closed. When we got back to the hotel, at around 3 a.m., he proposed to me. He didn't have a ring or anything, but I think I remember him getting to his knees, or maybe falling to his knees, and

I was like, *Oh, my God! Yes! That's so awesome!*

When I woke up the next morning, hungover as hell, I didn't totally remember what had happened. Apparently, I was engaged! My fiancé was already awake and on the phone with his parents. He was like, "Oh, my God! Yes! Ashley said yes! I'm so excited."

I thought to myself, *You know, this guy is so nice and I love his family, so let's just see what happens.*

About ten months later, we were married. It was puppy love, and we were young and hopeful. I think maybe he was the first really nice guy I'd ever been with. Plus, his family was absolutely terrific, and they loved him, so I decided to love him too.

This period of my life holds an important lesson for all you women out there: When you marry someone, you have to marry them *exactly as they are.* You can't marry the *idea* of the man. That guy there, that's what you're going to get, and it's *all* you're going to get. He's not going to change, to suddenly become *more* than he is now. That shit ain't going to get better. So I learned my lesson, the hard way: Marriage is a legal contract; it ain't always about love.

DURING THIS TIME, I met who I thought was a very cool New York fashion designer through an extremely pretentious interior decorator, and he loved my work, and that helped distract me from my seriously challenging marriage.

When the designer told me he wanted to host a show for me in New York City, I almost plotzed. *New York City! Seriously?* I was

AT ONE POINT, A GUY FROM SECURITY CAME UPSTAIRS, KNOCKED ON MY DOOR, AND ASKED IF I WAS OKAY. "YES," I SAID, AND I SMILED A LUNATIC SMILE. "I'M FINE. I'M JUST CRYING."

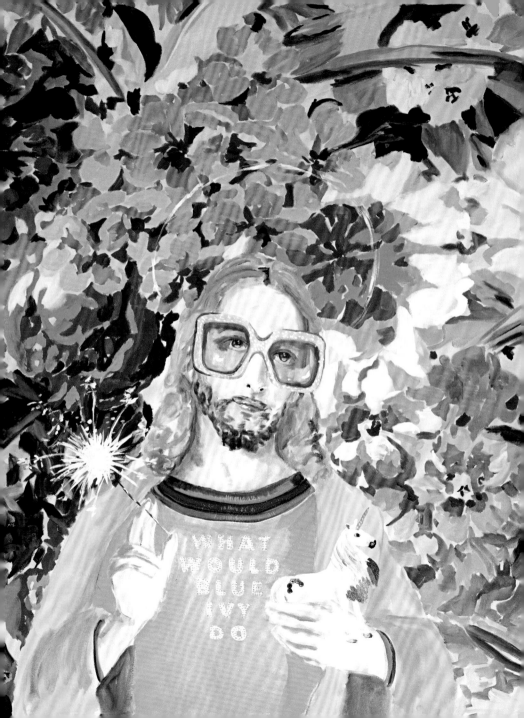

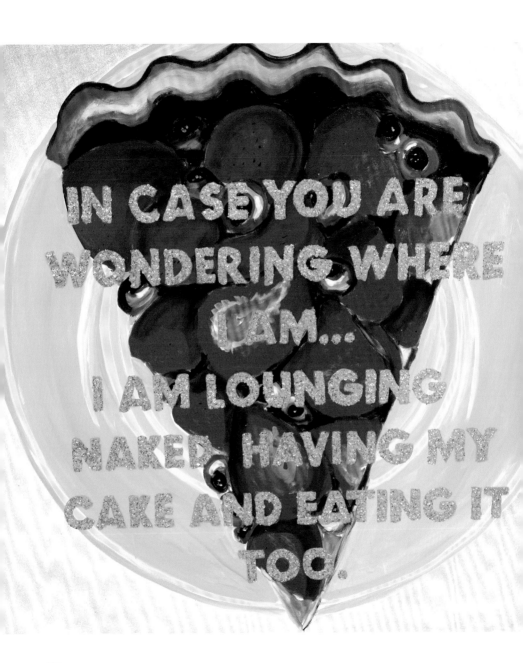

IN CASE YOU ARE WONDERING WHERE I AM... I AM LOUNGING NAKED, HAVING MY CAKE AND EATING IT TOO.

a young, naive artist; I didn't realize that New York was a whole 'nother fucking ballgame. The highs are really high, but the lows can be really fucking low.

I arrived at this designer's huge, trendy, downtown apartment and was blown away. I had never really been exposed to a world like that before. The designer took me for lunch at Cipriani downtown, a restaurant where all the Wall Street guys hung out and told each other how rich they were, I guess. One of his friends, a hedge-fund guy, had taken a liking to my art and had sent out an email to all of his equally moneyed-up buddies telling them about this hot, young artist from New Orleans. Suddenly, my phone started ringing off the hook, and there were people on the other end who wanted to give me money for my paintings. At the time, I thought it was all the money in the world.

I had never, ever, ever thought I could make that much fucking money in my life! I was in shock. I excused myself from lunch and went outside to smoke a cigarette and bawl my goddamn eyes out, right underneath a huge statue of a bull. The Maître d' came over to check on me, and I told him, through my tears, how excited I was to finally be making it. He looked me up and down and said, "Darling! You are the Matadora of New York City!" Right then, I felt the rush of New York City. It's like a drug. I thought that things could only get better at the event being thrown for me later that night.

I WAS WRONG. It couldn't have gone worse. I, of course, had no idea that I was going to have to pay for everything myself, including shipping and storage, and assorted "fees." "Oh, Ash," my designer friend nonchalantly asked me, "you wouldn't mind going to pick up the catering would you?" He failed to mention I'd also be picking up the bill. I was furious at myself for being sucked into this game, but when showtime rolled around, I put on my happy, confident face and went out to meet the fans.

I didn't sell a thing—I didn't even like the vacuous people who showed up, mostly for the wine, I guess, which I had also paid for—and when I got back to the hotel, I couldn't stop crying. Every dime I had made that day had gone to putting on this asshole designer's event. At one point, a guy from security came upstairs, knocked on my door, and asked if I was okay. "Yes," I said, and

WHEN YOU MARRY SOMEONE, YOU HAVE TO MARRY THEM *EXACTLY AS THEY ARE*. YOU CAN'T MARRY THE *IDEA* OF THE MAN.

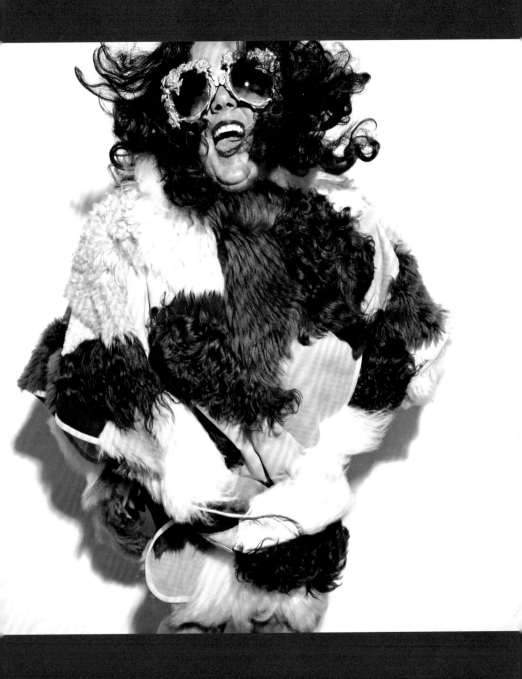

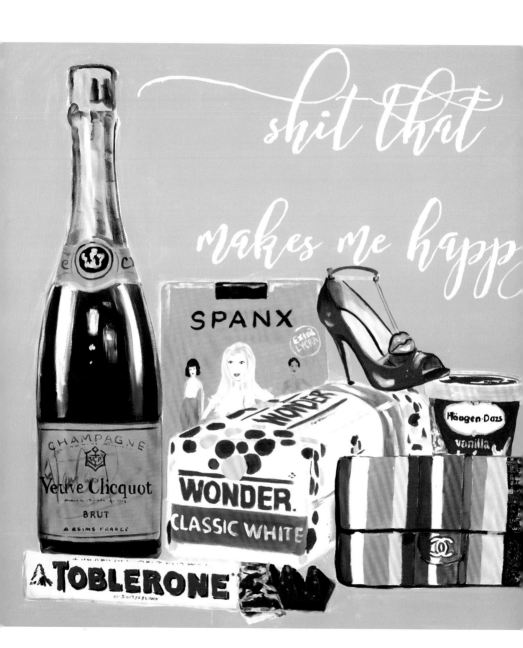

I smiled a lunatic smile. "I'm fine. I'm just crying."

I had learned an important lesson. All that glitters is not gold. No one was going to look out for me but myself. I went back to New Orleans, determined to be stronger. I spent endless hours in my little studio, painting away, and more hours in front of my computer, marketing myself. Everything else in my life began to fade away, and I was blindly focused on my success as an artist. Unsurprisingly, this is not the best recipe for making a marriage work.

I was determined to be the world's best artist, and I wasn't feeling as excited about becoming the world's best wife. All I wanted to do was paint, and get my art out into the world. Deep in my heart, I knew this marriage was over, but I wasn't ready to give up on love.

In the lifecycle of an entrepreneur, there are ups and downs; there are failures and successes. You don't give up on your career because of one business failure, and you don't give up on love because you get into the wrong relationship. You keep pushing forward, no matter what. And I'm lucky I did, because the end of this tunnel was the light of my life—I just didn't know it yet.

The following week, when my husband left for work, I went to pick up the U-Haul I'd reserved, returned to the house, packed up my worldly possessions, and went to visit friends in Birmingham, Alabama, just in time for a Josh Rouse concert, and I never looked back.

I was determined to be the world's best artist, and I wasn't feeling as excited about becoming the world's best wife.

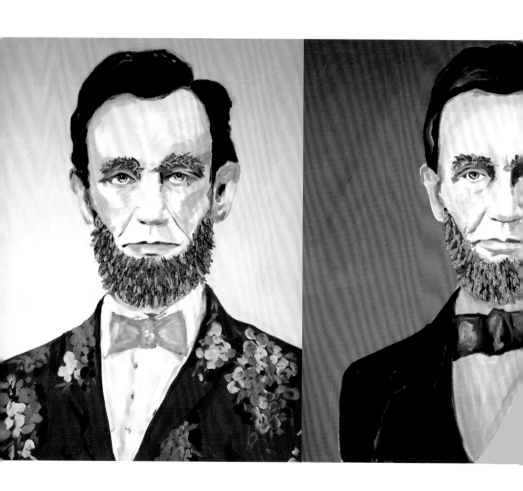

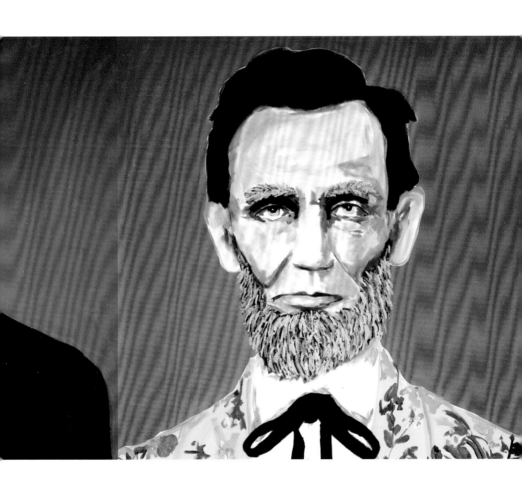

7
When You Know, You Know

IT WAS AN EASY DIVORCE.
I gave him back the diamond. All I wanted was my freedom so I could focus on my art. If I wanted another diamond, I figured I'd buy one for myself . . . eventually. Lord knows a diamond ain't worth getting married for.

I spent four or five days in Birmingham, then I went back to New Orleans and stayed with a friend until I could find a place to live. I still had my little studio, so I painted every day, but here's the real shit-kicker: My friend had a brother I'd never met, a photographer, going through a divorce, and he was living in her little guesthouse. I really don't know how to explain this part of my story, except that great magic and unexplainable wonder can happen on any damn day. And the day I met my friend's brother in the guesthouse? That was the day that I met the love of my life.

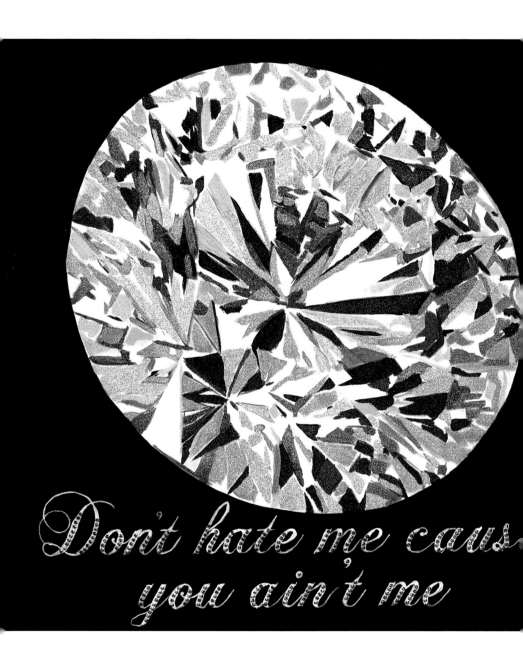

Don't hate me caus you ain't me

If I wanted another diamond, I figured I'd buy one for myself . . . eventually. Lord knows a diamond ain't worth getting married for.

I mean, the guy was handsome, but I'm not *that* shallow. It's more like I had a chemical reaction to his presence, and I could feel my hormones pinballing around like crazy, leaving me weak and light-headed and, okay, horny. That's when I finally understood all those *National Geographic* specials I'd seen as a child, where the lions see each other and go completely nuts, and they fuck like college kids on spring break, because it's all about procreating. I wasn't sure I wanted children, mind you, but my body was telling me I should go through the motions.

Of course, being a Southern lady, I didn't want to rush into anything, and I was able to exercise a modicum of self-control. But a few nights later, still smitten and hormonal as all fuck, I went outside, sat on the stoop, looked up at the heavens, and said, "Universe, give me a sign." At that precise moment, I saw the biggest shooting star I'd ever seen in my life, so I walked over to the guesthouse, up the steps, and laid it on him, and a week later we were living together. The same powerful feeling I had in my gut that told me that my first marriage was over was telling me this time it was *right*.

That was ten years ago, and Michael is still my man. And we're idiotically happy.

Things moved pretty quickly. Hey, when you know, you know, right? But, my divorce wasn't even final and my dad was a little concerned. "What do you mean you've already met somebody else?" I assured my dad we were fine. We were like a lesbian couple: One week into our relationship, and we were ready to pack up the U-Haul and spend the rest of our lives together.

Michael and I, it is *true love.* And it taught me a valuable lesson. When I was younger, looking for "Mr. Right," I was filled with angst. I'd meet guys, but nothing ever felt quite right. Then I found Michael, and I knew immediately that this was the person I was meant to be with, and that we were going to have an amazing life together, and instead of angst, I was filled with energy and hope. My life was finally coming together, and fueled by the confidence that came with my new relationship, my art really took on another dimension.

I'd been raised to look for a man to take care of me. A guy who would pay the bills, buy me a car, get me a first-class seat on the airplane. I had never wanted that, though; I had always assumed that I would take care of myself. And with Michael, I finally understood it. We were going to *take care of each other.* We were together for the right reasons. Not money, not luxury, not social climbing . . . love!

Yeah, I know—I get it. I sound like one of those sappy greeting cards you find at Walgreens. *You Complete Me.* (Or was that a Julia Roberts movie?) But it's true. I'm a modern woman. I can take care of my own damn self.

Michael and I are a team. Behind every woman is an even better man. He wants me to be happy, and he wants me to be fulfilled in my work. He's good with a hammer and helps me around the gallery. He photographs my art. And sometimes in the middle of the day, when I'm lost in my work, he'll show up with an incredible homemade lunch. And you know what? Sometimes I cry. Not just because the lunch is so good, which it is, but because he makes it all right for me not to be strong all the time. With Michael by my side, I don't have to pretend I'm some kind of superwoman.

WE WERE LIKE A LESBIAN COUPLE: ONE WEEK INTO OUR RELATIONSHIP, AND WE WERE READY TO PACK UP THE U-HAUL AND SPEND THE REST OF OUR LIVES TOGETHER.

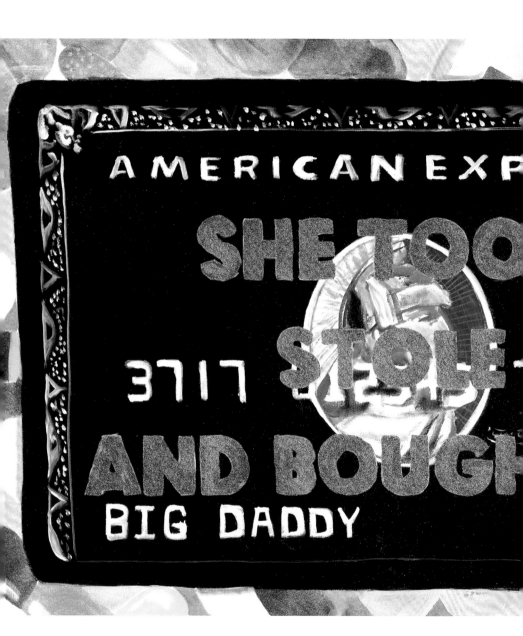

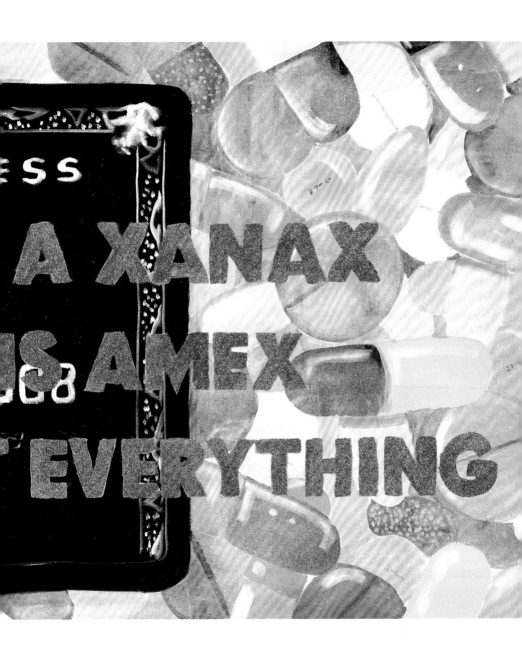

8
Superhero Artist Vibes

MEANWHILE, BACK AT MY studio, my baller artist vibes were in full force. I was starting to build up a bit of a collector base, and my voice was really growing stronger as an artist. The experience of overcoming failure had really boosted my confidence. So, I decided to treat myself to some time with the ladies. One of my clients invited me to lunch with a bunch of local socialites, potential new clients, and it dragged on for three hours. Every time one of them got up to pee, all the other women began talking shit about her. "The whole town knows her husband's having an affair." "If I were her, I'd sue that plastic surgeon." "She's got two boys, and one is weirder than the next. Maybe that look-alike husband of hers is actually her brother."

I swear to God, I was so scared to leave the table I gave myself a bladder infection. I guess it was worth it—I sold a couple of

WHILE WE WERE WAITING FOR THE VALET TO BRING THEIR FANCY CARS, ALL I HEARD WAS: "DO I LOOK FAT? REALLY, DO I LOOK FAT?" AND I'M THINKING, "YOU DON'T LOOK FAT, YOU LOOK CRAZY!"

paintings—but now I'm mostly scared to do those kinds of lunches. I guess I could always wear Depends, like that woman astronaut.

But here's the thing. That lunch gave me fodder. Why did these women have to be so mean? And the shit they worried about! Every last one of them was on a diet, picking at her food like a bird, and it got to a point where I just wanted to mind my own business and take the food right off their plates.

While we were waiting for the valet to bring their fancy cars, all I heard was: "Do I look fat? Really, do I look fat?" And I'm thinking, "You don't look fat, you look crazy!"

I knew that instant that I had to go home and paint that. And that's exactly what I did. And I wasn't being *mean,* like some of them; I was, in fact, making the world a better place by holding up a mirror to these women so they could get some sense and stop torturing themselves and each other.

You ever watch any of that *Real Housewives* bullshit? It's a bunch of really angry, emaciated women who've been waxed, lasered, and plucked to within an inch of their lives, who spend every waking moment trying not to eat. You know why they're angry? Because they're *hungry.* Don't fucking do that to yourself.

AFTER THAT encounter, more socially conscious work followed. I did a whole series inspired by hedge-fund billionaires. I had a close-up of Benjamin Franklin on the dollar bill, wearing a red clown nose, with the words "I'll Make You Hollar for a Dollar" stamped across the front. Another said, "Always Ask for More." And still another said "Mine Is Bigger

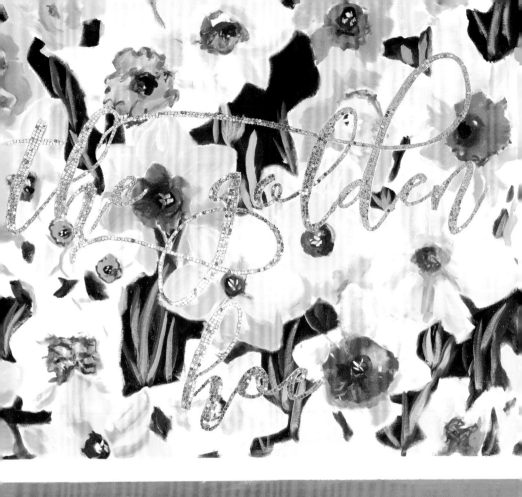

the Golden Hoe

THE ART OF BEING A MUCH BIGGER HOE THAN THE AVERAGE HOE

Ashley Longshore

The Garden Club Exposed

DOUBLE comma MOMMA

The Secrets of the Birkin Brigade

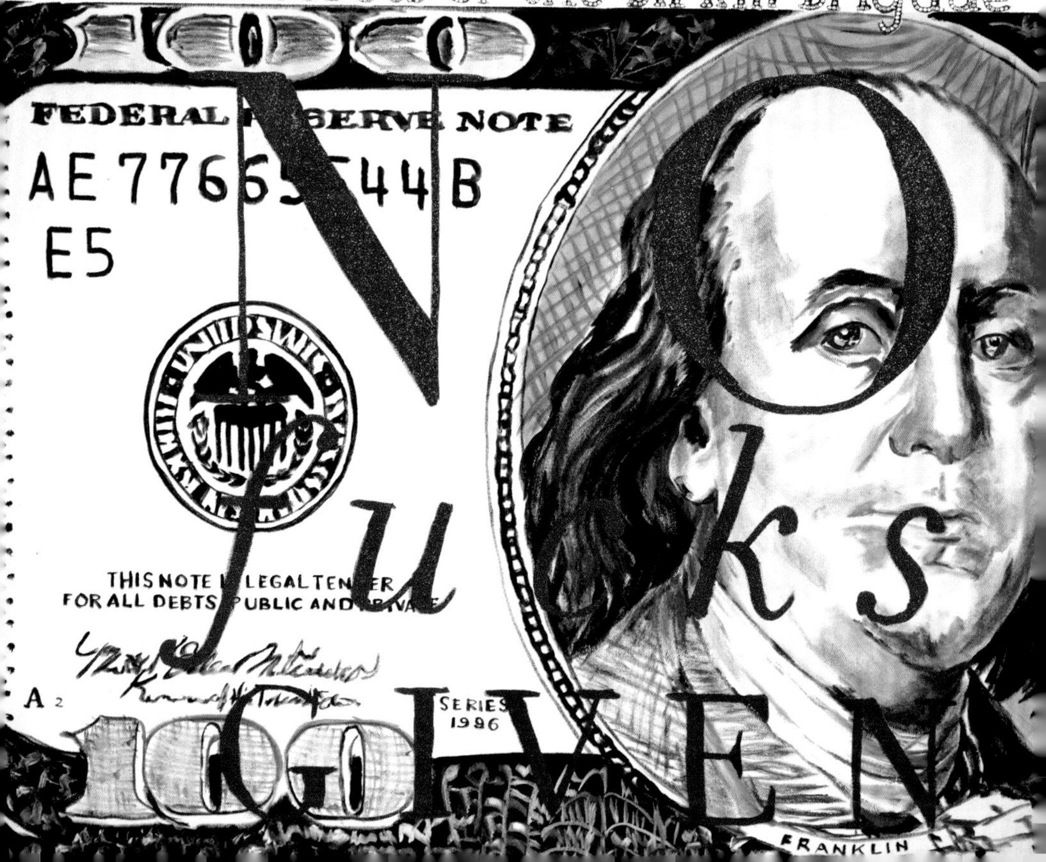

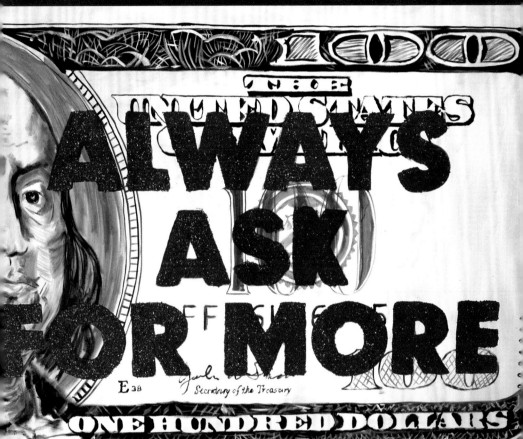

Than Yours." But my very favorite was "How to Win Friends and Secure Major Poontang."

I painted a grown man on a tricycle with the words "The Bugatti Has a Flat and the Jet Is Out of Fuel. Now What?" as a statement on American success. So many people spend every dime they make just to show how much money they have. And the minute that shit isn't perfect and the money ain't flowin' like Dom Pérignon, they hightail it out of there. They're all flash and no substance.

Guess who bought those paintings. All the hedge-fund guys. Thank you, you filthy rich guys, for sharing your wealth with a needy artist such as me. You guys are okay. And we're not that different, you and I. Remember what Andy Warhol said? "Being good in business is the most fascinating kind of art. Making money is art and working is art, and good business is the best art."

Then I began to travel and really see the world. I went overseas to Europe and India, and it made me appreciate this great country that much more. Most countries treat their women like shit, often in the name of religion, and those experiences inspired my *Holy Fuck!* series. I have nothing but the utmost respect for religion—all religion—but it's bullshit that it's used as an excuse to treat women like second-class citizens and worse just because men are threatened by our strength and beauty.

I was inspired to paint Kate Moss as a nun. She was covered in a habit, but she was still Kate Moss, still beautiful, and that was the message: Instead of relegating women to the shadows, you should be celebrating them.

It pissed me off. Women gave birth to you. Raised you. And this is how you show your appreciation? Motherhood is some powerful shit. Women are not getting their due. This is very wrong. No one should be devalued because of their genitalia.

As it happened, I was thinking these deep thoughts on National Woman's Day, so I posted a little something on Instagram: "Here's to all the mothers out there. I have

None of us is perfect. We all make mistakes. And we're all trying to make sense of this business of living.

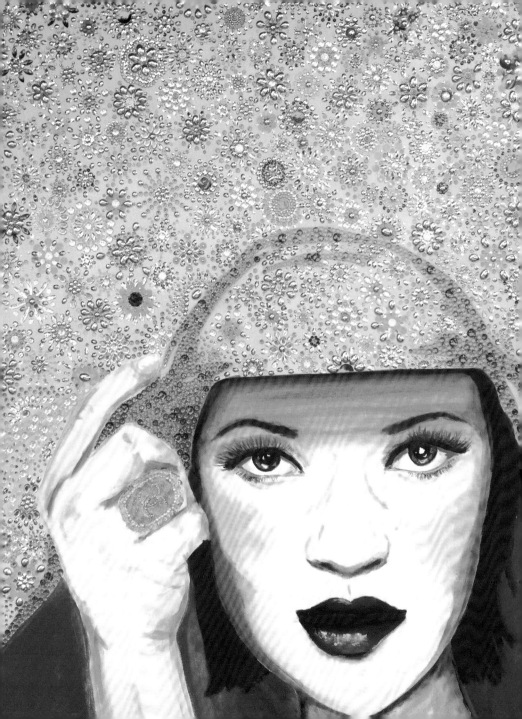

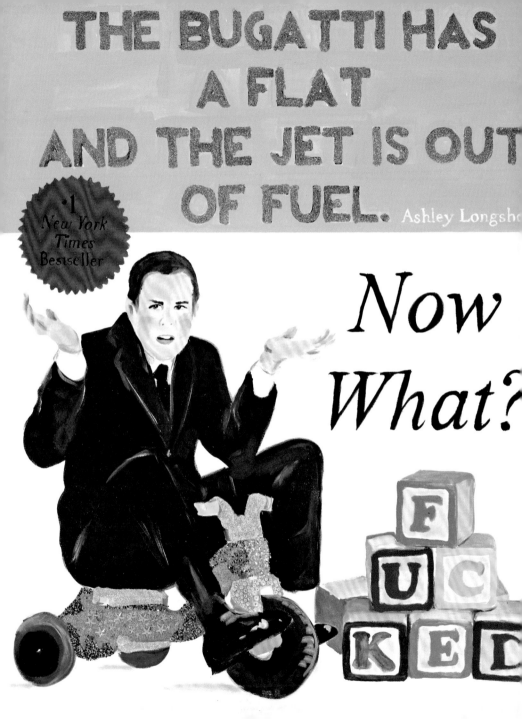

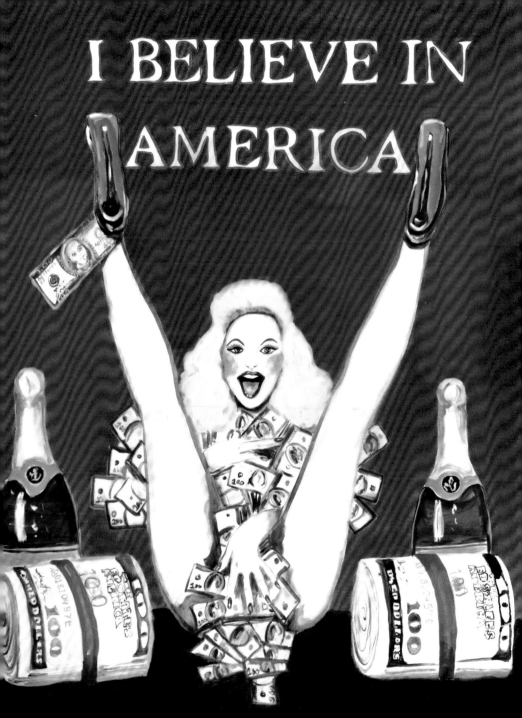

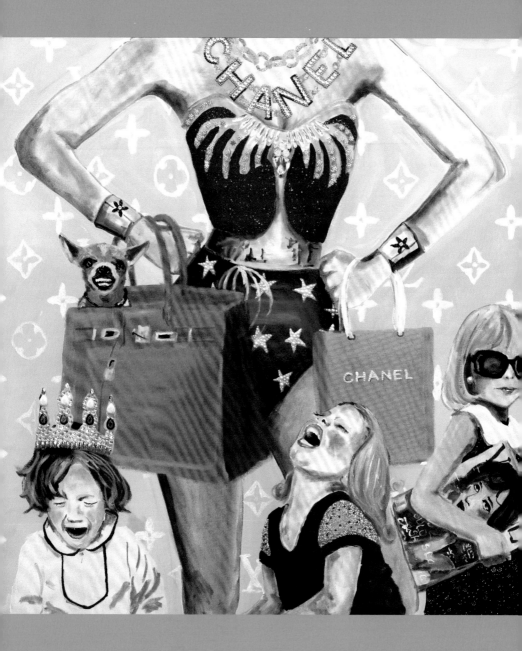

THE GREATEST
MENTORS I HAVE
HAD ARE MOTHERS.
THEY ARE BADASS
BITCHES, BOSSES, AND
WONDER WOMEN.

so much respect for you. I don't know how you have the time to do all that you do. You are an inspiration to me."

Almost immediately, an angry woman wrote back: "Why do you hate women so much? Why don't you understand that there are millions of women who haven't chosen the same route as you? Why do you make fun of women who wear workout clothes? Or who take Pilates? Or who like pretty things!"

I was like, *I can't believe this.* I was trying to say something nice, something supportive to a group of women I admire and respect. The greatest mentors I have had are mothers. They are badass bitches, bosses, and Wonder Women. Motherhood is supremely hard, and I'm only guessing, because I'm not a mother. After eighteen years of hell, your kid goes off to college and doesn't even answer your texts! Uh-oh. That is so not right.

But this angry woman wouldn't stop. "You mock us, and you know nothing about us!"

Mock you?! Lady, I'm not mocking anybody. I'm trying to understand the world around me. Forgive me if I do it with a sense of humor, which clearly you don't have. I have society ladies coming into my studio and looking at paintings of society ladies *just like*

themselves, and they buy them. Why? Because they get it. They have a sense of humor.

None of us is perfect. We all make mistakes. And we're all trying to make sense of this business of living.

I'm not criticizing. I'm observing. I'm creating. And creating makes me happy. When I paint, I express myself. When someone buys one of my paintings, they are not only acknowledging my right to express myself, they are telling me that they like what I have to say. This is a very intimate relationship. By hanging my painting on your wall, you're basically living with me . . . well, at least with my *spirit.* We have something in common now—we are family. Does it get any better than that? I think not.

And not to get all existential on your asses, but I think all of us have an innate need to communicate, to connect. It's hard out there, and doubly hard when you're alone. When I paint, I'm listening to my inner voice, putting my feelings on the canvas, and reaching out. That's what art is about, *communicating.* Hell, that's what *life* is about.

I paint from the inside. My paintings are bold, bright, opulent, defiant, and—yes—snarky. But people don't seem to mind.

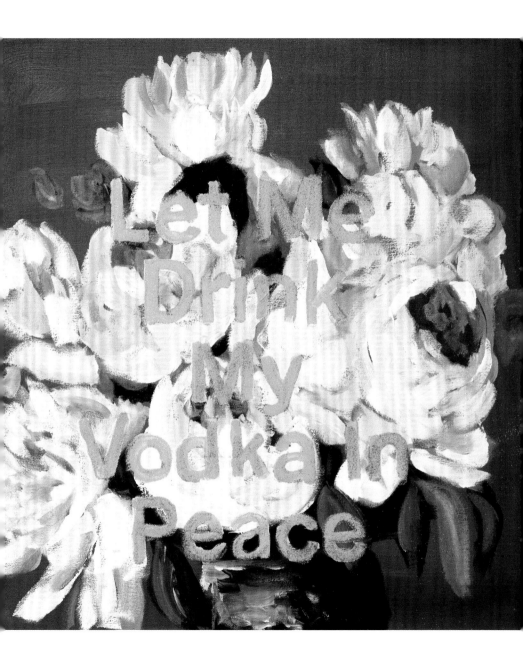

9
Carpe Diem, Bitches

ABOUT TWO YEARS AGO, shit started happening in earnest. I got a call from *Forbes* magazine; they liked my work. Anthropologie, the big retailer, was doing a massive project in Portugal, and they wanted me to be part of it. The Cornell Museum gave me a show, *Bling. Art That Shines.* I got a call from the Bryant Park Hotel, in New York, asking if I would help them create an "Ashley Longshore Suite" for New York Fashion Week. Hello?! *Are you fucking kidding me?!* A few weeks later, I arrived in Manhattan with a truckload of paintings.

Millions of people showed up at the Bryant Park Hotel (okay, I'm exaggerating just a little) to check out the Ashley Longshore Suite. And when I got back to New Orleans, feeling justifiably giddy but working hard not to let it go to my head, I got a call from a local cinematographer. He was doing a movie in New Orleans with Salma Hayek, and she had developed an interest in painting when she starred in that Frida Kahlo film, which was called, curiously enough, *Frida.* Salma had seen my work and she wanted to meet, and he was having a little party at his house on Saturday. "Are you free?" he asked.

Well, let's see. I'm free Tuesday, Wednesday, Thursday—and every night for the rest of my life.

Not long after, I'm sitting in my studio with the gorgeous Salma Hayek, walking her through the paces, talking it through. "I work in layers, Salma. May I call you Salma? First I paint the image, in acrylic, because I'm impatient, and acrylic dries fast. Then I add glitter, gloss, shine, and sparkle. I like to go big. I like my work to be over the top. Just like I am."

My brush with beautiful, successful celebrities didn't end here. A year later, Blake Lively floated into my New Orleans studio. Now she is one of my biggest collectors. As a fellow artist, she understands the process and the artistry and appreciates me the way one kick-ass successful woman appreciates another. I even taught her how to paint, and let me tell you, she is not just a gorgeous, talented actress. Girl knows her colors!

AT THE END of the day, I work this hard because I like to express myself, but also because my true definition of success is the ability to take care of myself. I work hard so I don't ever have to ask anyone for a goddamn thing. So I don't have to suck a dick for anything in my life. I suck it 'cause I want to, not 'cause I have to.

I like to buy myself nice shit, and I have more than my fair share of designer purses. I like to go to Paris for a weekend to walk along the Seine eating macarons. And I'd love to visit Girona, Spain, and have dinner at El Celler de Can Roca, which is supposed to be the best restaurant in the world (this week).

What I'd really love is to have my own private jet, and I'm not talking a tin can, either—I need a Gulfstream G650ER Challenger, or a Bombardier Challenger. Something with serious range, so I can roll with my people. I'd call it Thunderpussy. It would be cherry red—that sparkly red that looks good on lowriders. And I'd paint the tail-wing myself, a black pussycat with a lighting bolt through it. And whenever *Thunderpussy* would come in for a landing, breaking through the clouds, people would look up at the sky and point and say, "Oh,

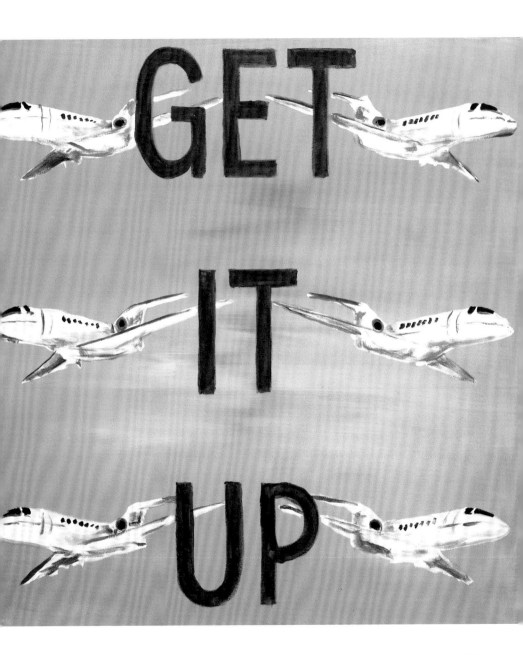

YOU'VE GOT TO WANT IT SO BADLY YOU NEVER STOP PUSHING YOURSELF. SOMETIMES TO THE POINT OF MADNESS.

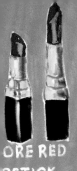

ORE RED
PSTICK

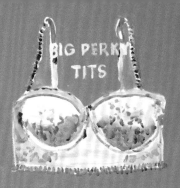

BIG PERKY
TITS

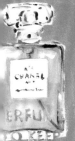

ERFUME
TO KEEP
GAR DADDY
TERESTED

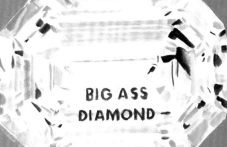

BIG ASS
DIAMOND →

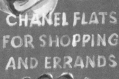

CHANEL FLATS
FOR SHOPPING
AND ERRANDS

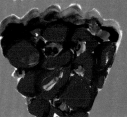

EATS FRENCH DESSERTS,
GAINS NO WEIGHT

CENTURION
CARD
AND
COPIOUS
SPENDING

3717   0009

SUPER PUSSY

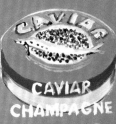

CAVIAR
CHAMPAGNE
COCAINE

XANAX
1.0

KIDS

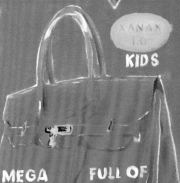

MEGA
BITCH
BAG

FULL OF
CASH
RITALIN
AND EXLAX

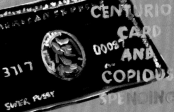

CK ME
HEELS

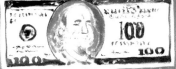

100

100

TIP FOR THE DOORMAN

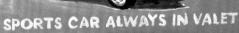

SPORTS CAR ALWAYS IN VALET

my God! It's *Thunderpussy*. Ashley Longshore is here!"

That feels right. That's worth working hard as fuck for.

But for the record, hard work becomes a lot easier when you love what you do.

And it's possible, people.

From the moment I picked up a paintbrush, back in my dorm in Montana, I identified as an artist. I decided it was my calling, and I never wavered. When I started painting, I was self-taught. I didn't take lessons. I didn't read *The Complete Idiot's Guide to Painting*. I sat down and worked until I did it. And now there's only one Ashley Longshore.

I had to go through hell to get here, and I still have days when I can't get out of bed. It's not all wine and roses, people. I still struggle. I still have doubts. And even now, with things humming along, with the machinery in high gear, there is still shit to take care of. It's great to be doing well, but I have to keep working, even when I'm not at my best. Yeah, I get the blues from time to time, but the show must go on. You don't get a spread in *Vogue* by whining. You do it by dragging your ass out of bed, even on the bad days, and getting your shit together. And when the next bad day comes along, you do a little yoga and try to meditate for your full twenty minutes without cheating, and you drag your sorry ass to the studio. That's the way it's done, people. I don't know any other way. And I'll tell you this: It's working for me. More often than not, I feel really fucking good about the life I've created for myself. I'm like a steam train with a paintbrush. I keep fighting the good fight, because that's what it's about. Doing good work. Producing. Creating.

You have to grab life by the balls. You have to do it. Nobody really gives a shit about your hopes and dreams. The sooner you come to terms with that, the more likely you are to succeed.

You've got to want it. *Badly.* You've got to want it so badly you never stop pushing yourself. Sometimes to the point of madness.

That also happens to be the Secret of Life: *You fall down; you get up. It's that simple—trust me.*

Carpe diem, bitches. Fuck yeah.

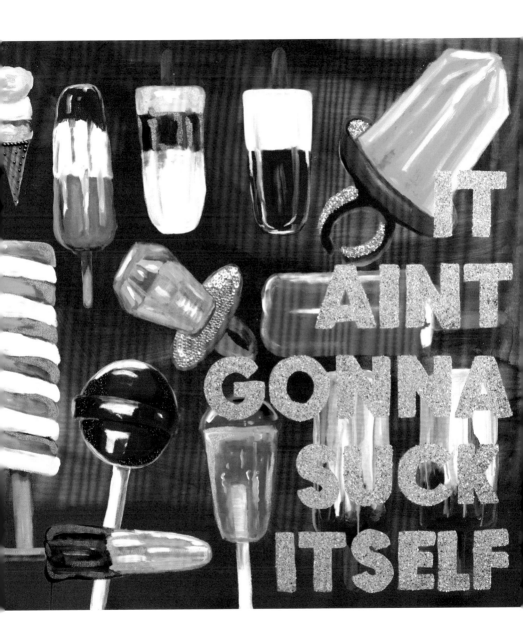

10
The A–Z of Being Ambitchous

ANNA WINTOUR: "I WOULD FUCK ME"

Sometimes I think that everything we do is about being fuckable. The dresses we wear, the purse we carry, the high-heels we stuff our feet into, the right plastic surgeon to hack up our faces. It's sad. I think every girl should look in the mirror every morning and say, "I would fuck me." It's a great way to start the day. Maybe I should put that on a greeting card. That's what it says on the front. Then you open it and it says, "But I wouldn't fuck you."

ART

I love art. I love artists. I want all artists to succeed. Art makes the world a better place. Please do your part; feed your local artists; help them make their rent. Without art, the world would be a dull and lonely place. Know them, love them, embrace them, support them.

ASSHOLES

Got no use for them. This one rich guy I sort of knew—I hadn't seen him in a while—he read about me in a magazine, saw me on TV, and ended up coming to one of my shows in New York. He came over and said, "It looks like you're finally turning into somebody." And I thought, "No, asshole. I've always been somebody. But you—even with all that money—you're nobody." Ain't that the truth?

ASSHOLES, PART 2

Bleaching. Not my thing. The asshole is not on the menu. But you go right ahead.

BENJAMIN "BENJI" FRANKLIN

To me, Benji is the biggest pop icon of success. That image on the hundred-dollar bill says so much about American greed, which is why billionaires and hedgies love him. What I don't get is: How do you get on the hundred-dollar bill with a face like that? Well, I did a painting of him wearing a shirt that says "Moose Cock," because even though I know the real reason he's on the hundred-dollar bill is that he did a big deal with France that made us a ton of money, in my mind, it was because he had a huge dick.

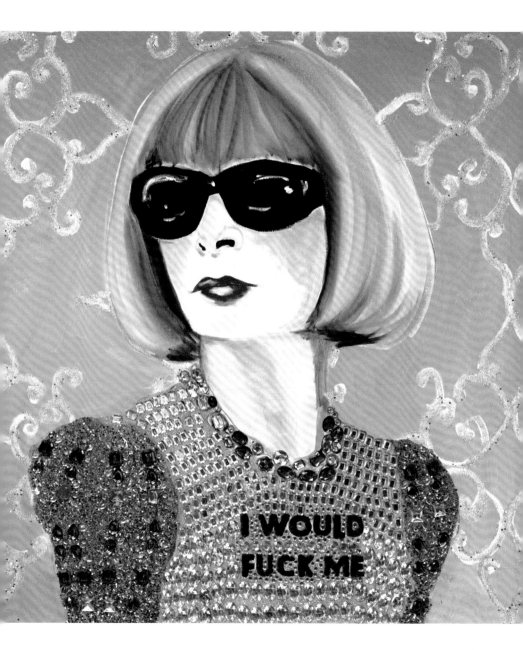

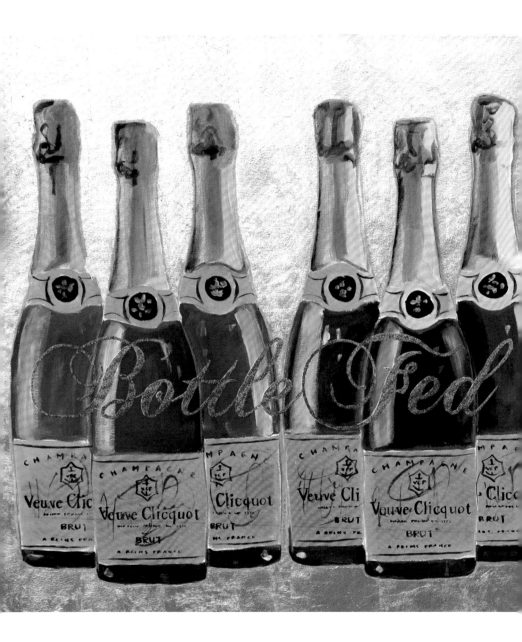

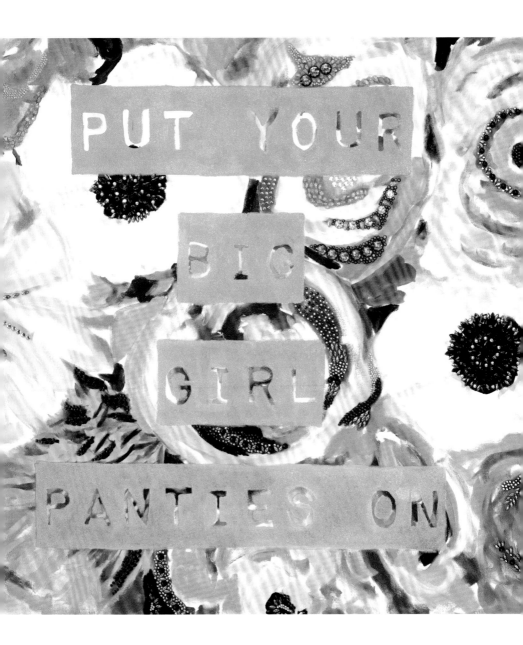

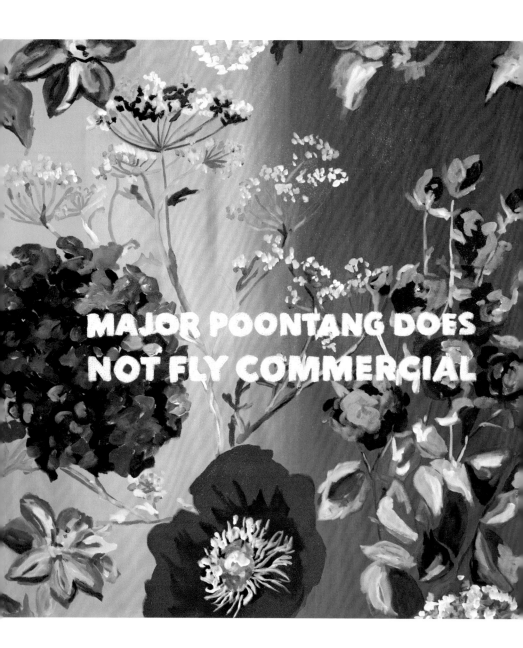

"No, asshole. I've always been somebody. But you—even with all that money—you're nobody."

"BIG GIRL PANTIES"

The message here is very simple. Stop complaining about that rich asshole you married. Stop complaining about your fake friends. Stop complaining about your ungrateful kids. Stop complaining, period. Just *woman* the fuck up, put on your big girl panties, and deal with it. And do it now, because one day it'll be too late. We all need a fucking purpose. Just get on with it.

"BITCHOPOTAMUS"

That's the biggest bitch in the room. That's the one I'm looking at. That's the queen bee. But if she comes to my show and whips out a black AmEx card, I'll forgive her anything.

"BOTTLE FED"

Veuve Cliquot is one of my favorite Champagnes. So is Billecart-Salmon. And so is anything that doesn't taste like rat piss with bubbles. Champagne makes a statement. "I've arrived, bitches." I also happen to like Champagne. So, sometimes it's not just about status. Sometimes drinking good champagne is really about drinking good champagne. And fuck a glass—it comes in one already!

CHRONIC MASTURBATION

I see trophy wives who don't have jobs or do anything with their lives, and I'm thinking, *What the fuck? You must be a chronic masturbator; that must be your excuse.* Honestly, that's the only excuse I'd really go for.

CRYING AT BERGDORF'S

There is no crying at Bergdorf's, and I know that because I did cry at Bergdorf's. I was shopping there, and I found some gorgeous clothes, and I went into the dressing room to try them on. Only there was not enough Lycra or Spanx in the world to make that shit fit me. So I got upset, first at myself because there's this list of shit that as a woman I should be doing in my life, like exercising so my waist is eighteen fucking inches around. And in this dressing room with awful lighting, I felt like I had failed. Sometimes when you're a woman, you just fucking crack, and that could be right in the middle of fucking Bergdorf's. But, really, are you shitting me with some of those sample sizes? They're for fucking Japanese babies. I'm a fucking woman; I have tits, okay?

"DOUBLE-COMMA MAMA"

I always said I wanted to be a double-comma mama. Hit that million-dollar mark. That shit is golden. Even though a million dollars ain't what it used to be, there's still something about making seven figures that must feel real good.

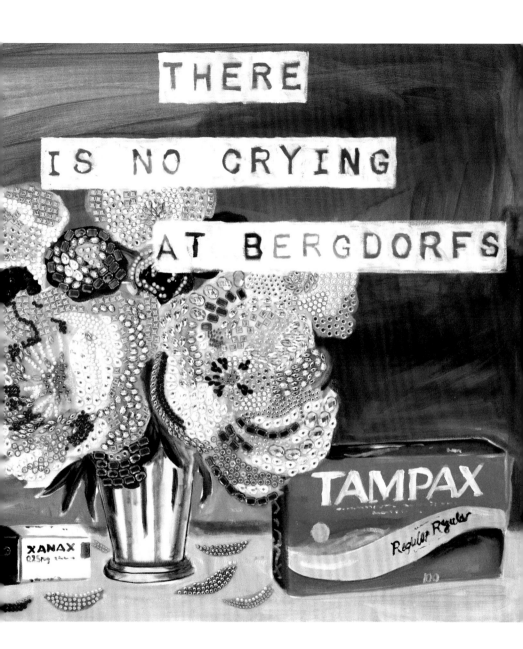

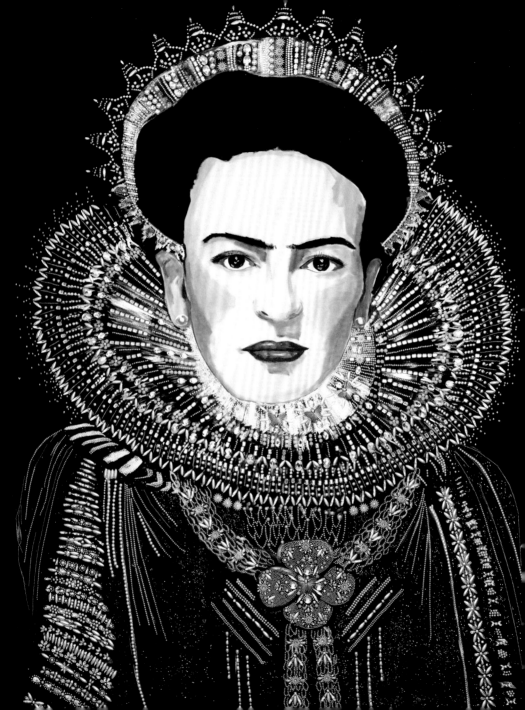

EXPECTATIONS

I've done enough highbrow shit; I've spent enough time at the Delano in Miami and Le Meurice in Paris to know that most of the shit you think is going to be fucking awesome ain't nothing but a fucking douchebag convention.

FEAR

Fear is good. (Greed, not so good. Times have changed.) I look back at the girl I was in Montana, twenty years ago now, and I realize I haven't changed that much. I'm still trying to find my way, still fearful, but I'm okay with it. I don't pretend I'm not afraid anymore. When you stop pretending, you have a lot more energy for life. Fear is a great catalyst for action, much better than revenge. When you confront your own fear, the world is at your fingertips. Sometimes the only one stopping you is yourself.

FEARLESS WOMEN

I love to paint women who inspire me with their beauty and strength. I have a whole series of Audrey Hepburn paintings, because to me she's the epitome of elegance. I've got Kate Moss in a nunnery. I've got Frida Kahlo looking as unfathomable as ever. I've got Beyoncé covered in flowers and birds, because she is so creatively inspiring, as a mother, a woman, and an artist, and I love her energy.

I love fearless women. Beautiful women. Confident women. I love women who know that at the end of the day, they're going to be a day older, and that they need to take advantage of every fucking minute. That's inspiring. To milk the hell out of life. That kind of passion and energy is what makes a woman beautiful. But it helps to be born with the right bone structure, too.

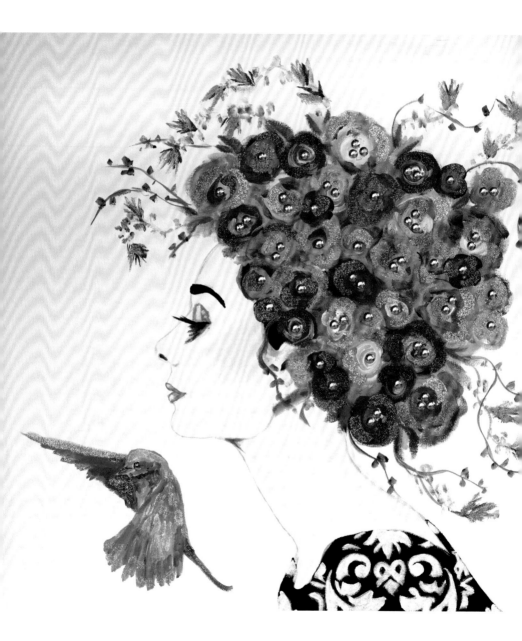

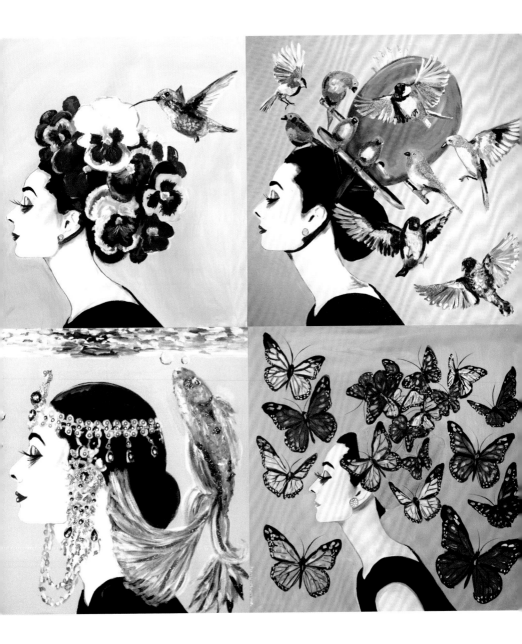

FEAR IS A GREAT CATALYST FOR ACTION, MUCH BETTER THAN REVENGE. WHEN YOU CONFRONT YOUR OWN FEAR, THE WORLD IS AT YOUR FINGERTIPS. SOMETIMES THE ONLY ONE STOPPING YOU IS YOURSELF.

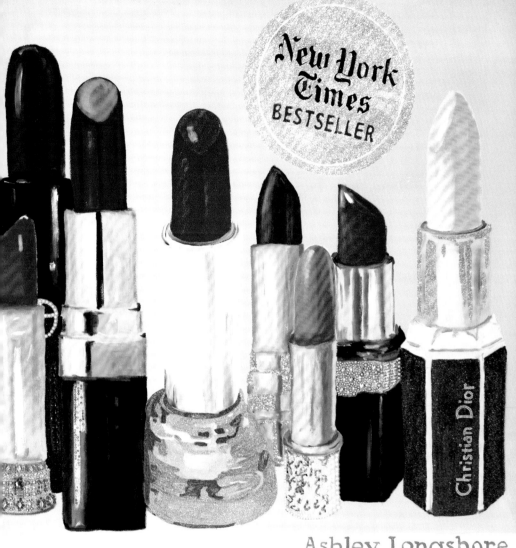

Ashley Longshore

this is a stick up

an action mystery novel about pussy stuff

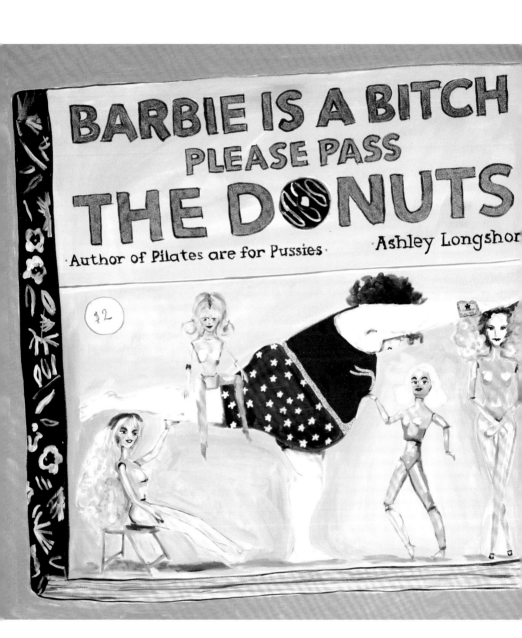

FEMALE MAINTENANCE

Here's the thing: Even after putting in a thirteen-hour day of meetings, calls, and painting, there's shit I'm supposed to do. I'm supposed to do cardio, I'm supposed to do yoga, I'm supposed to meditate, I'm supposed to get a fucking massage, I'm supposed to get lash extensions, get my mustache waxed, my chin waxed, my armpits lasered, get a fucking Brazilian so my pussy looks like it's smiling (from the side, anyway), shave my fucking legs, get manicured and fucking pedicured. AND, I'm supposed to do all of this and still have time to give my man a blowjob and have dinner with my friends. On second thought, no. Forget it. It's too exhausting. That's a full-time job in and of itself. Maybe I'll skip it today . . .

Once, I tried to take a shortcut, and I got a chemical burn from Nair. I was on my way to Jamaica and hadn't had time to get a wax, and I was like, *Jesus Christ, I can't go down to Jamaica with fucking steel wool hanging out, looking like I have a tennis ball in my suit* (you know, when your muff gets smashed down and it looks like a tennis ball?). So I was like, *Fuck it, I'll get some Nair,* and I was immediately like, *Goddamn, this hurts.* It literally removed all my skin down there, I was walking like Redd Fox, bowlegged, for days.

But fuck it, because here's the thing: When you find the right man who loves you, he ain't gonna turn it down, even when you've got a chemical burn.

FRIENDSHIP

I'm not into that whole Leo Buscaglia greeting-card bullshit ("A single rose can be my garden . . . a single friend, my world"), but I know this much: If you're not laughing, you need better friends.

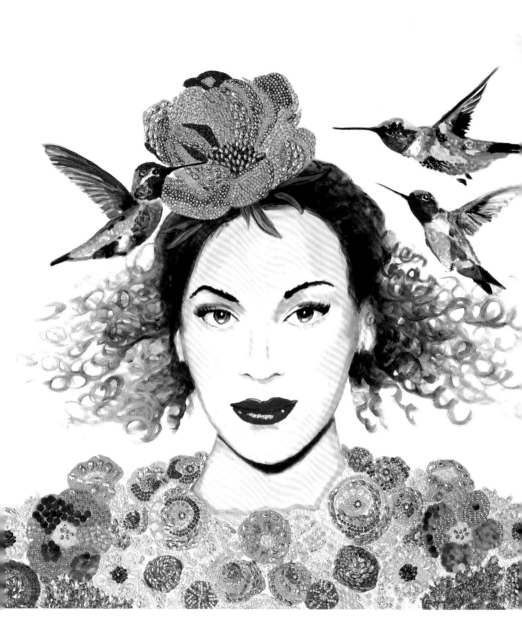

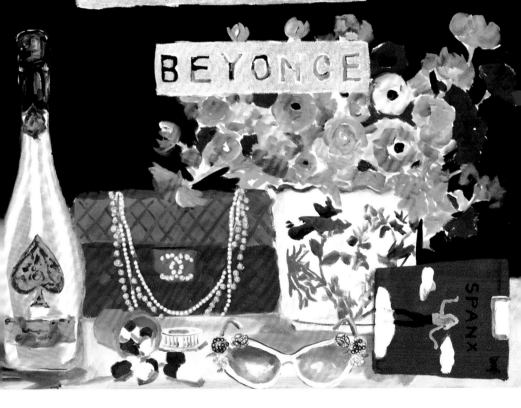

CRYING IN CHANEL

ISN'T VERY

BEYONCE

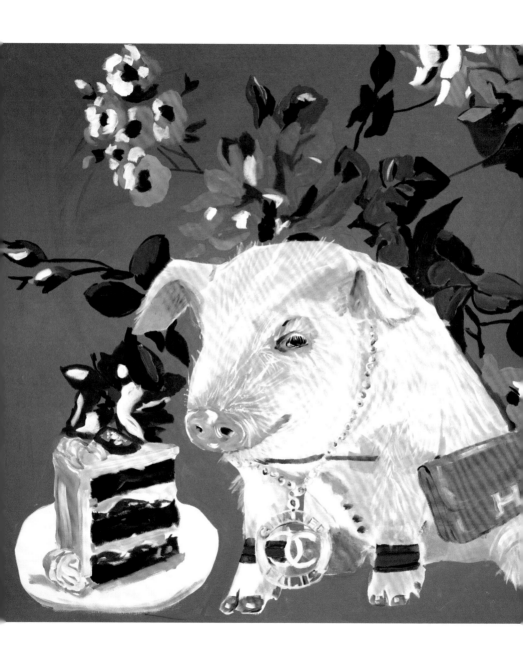

"FUCK THE GARDEN CLUB"

I'm so mesmerized by the idea of making planting flowers bitchy. These women have taken something as simple as planting ferns and made it a cunt-fest. Only upper-crust white women have the opportunity to do something like that. Is the Garden Club really about gardening? I don't know what the fuck it's about. There are women who are devastated to not be in the Garden Club, and I'm like, "Are you shitting me?! Do you really care about plants that much?!" Obviously not.

"THE GOLDEN HOE"

This is about being a much bigger hoe than the average ho. It's the Garden Club exposed. The Golden Hoe drives a range rover or a Mercedes SVU. The Golden Hoe wouldn't be seen dead without a pair of heels on, except *maybe* at the grocery store. The Golden Hoe is the chair of every big social event, but don't get it twisted, this prima donna can suck a mean dick. She would give a handjob for a Birkin bag in a minute, and she would beat that thing like she was mad at it. She is the most gorgeous woman you have ever seen . . . and she is as mean as a snake.

"GUCCI PIG"

I spent $6,000 on two pairs of gorgeous Gucci boots I had been lusting after, and I was thrilled when I finally found them online. I couldn't wait for them to arrive. When they did, I tore open the box, stuffed my feet into them, pulled up the zipper and . . . they didn't fit over my calves! The damn Gucci Pig was born right there.

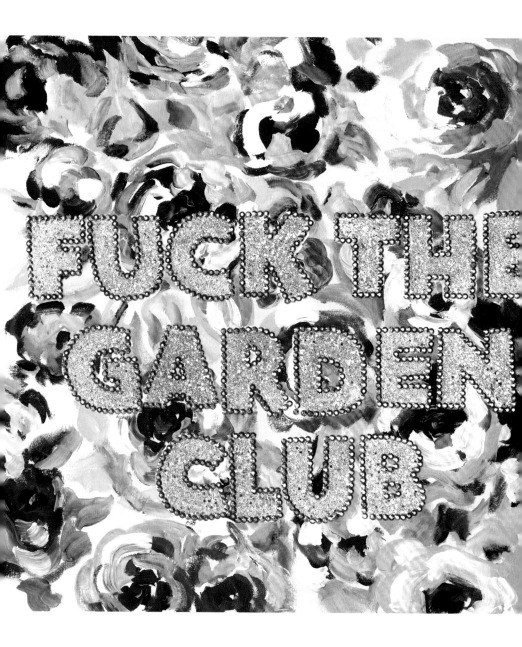

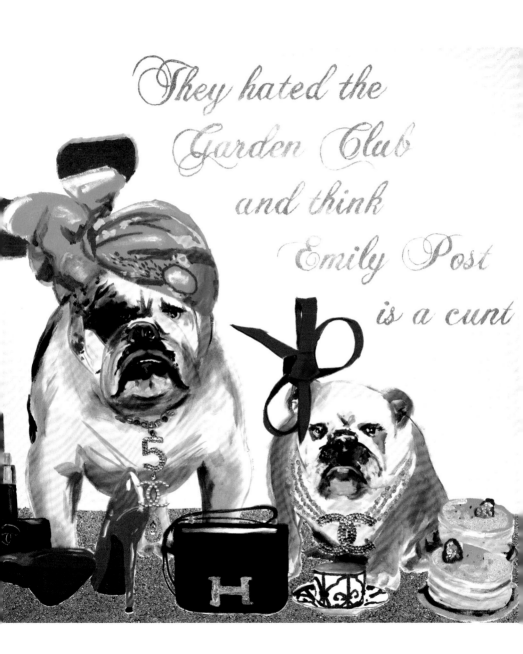

They hated the
Garden Club
and think
Emily Post
is a cunt

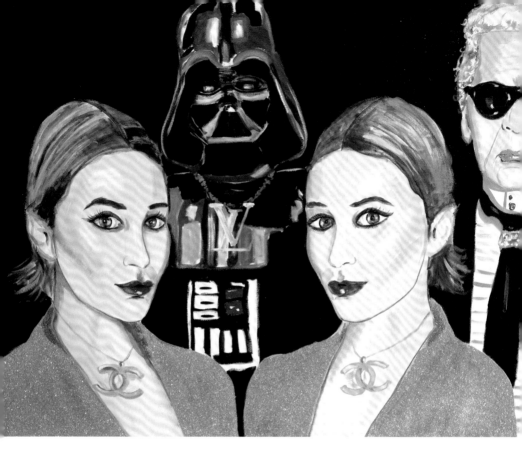

HAPPYGASMS

A combination of an orgasm, an artgasm, and a moneygasm. Honestly, if you put "gasm" at the end of anything, it works. But a happygasm is the best. It's when everything just feels right in the world. When my jeans don't feel tight, when I'm selling art, when I've had a *real* orgasm, when it's not too hot outside, when I'm feeling inspired, when all the people I love are okay, and when I couldn't literally give two fucks about anything else.

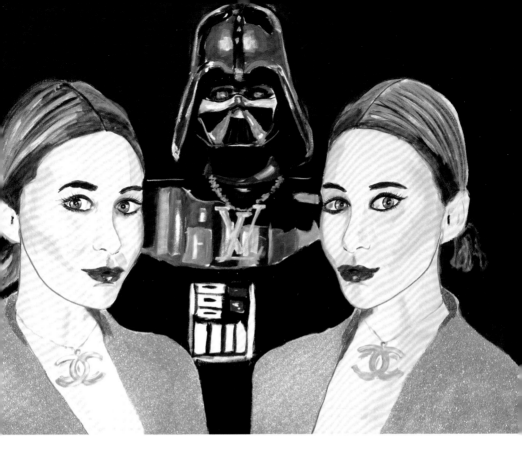

KARL LAGERFELD

Here's Karl Lagerfeld, front and center in *The Fashion Empire Strikes Back*. Karl is a modern emperor. He was a powerful force at both Chanel and Fendi, not to mention the label to which he lends his name. Maybe he should also add fat police to that title. Even though he got outed for stealing into a McDonald's for his favorite lunch, like a thief in the night. Come on, Karl! Nothing wrong with a double cheese, fries, and a Coke. No need to hide behind those big sunglasses. I loved you when you were fat, and I love you now that you're skinny. I'll take you any way I can get you.

KEGELS

This is not a choice. You've got to keep it tight. The best times to do Kegels are when you're eating carbs, or at the drive-thru at McDonald's, because if you're going to be curvy, then you might as well keep it tight. Or, when you're waiting in line. People will look at you funny in the bank, sure, but you're doing it for your man, so keep going. You're also doing it for yourself. Who wants to pee a little every time she sneezes? Are you doing Kegels now? Dudes need to do Kegels too, by the way; I learned this shit in Pilates.

KIM AND KANYE

Oh, look, it's Kanye on a box of Cocoa Puffs cereal, and Kim on a jug of milk. *Lunch Is for Pussies.* Why? I loved the idea of Kanye being all serious on the Cocoa Puffs box and Kim's cry face on a carton of milk, and if you mix the two of them together and they sit for too long—it becomes a whole disgusting mess that you have to choke down really quick. And with the way their egos are, if those two had each other for breakfast, why the fuck would they need lunch?

LOOKS CAN BE DECEIVING

Some women come to the studio with a $200,000 car, a seven-carat diamond on their finger, and a $10,000 handbag, and I'll think I'm about to hit gold. Then they'll pick out a $5,000 painting and ask if they can pay it off over the next six months. They have no fucking cash; it's all a façade. Then I have a woman rolling up in here in a Disney World sweatshirt and Crocs, and I'm thinking, "This chick looks as crazy as a shithouse rat," but I come to find that she's a millionaire. Makes you realize, when you've really got it, you don't have to prove a goddamn thing. Women don't have to prove anything if you work and make your own money; it's more about the cash than the flash.

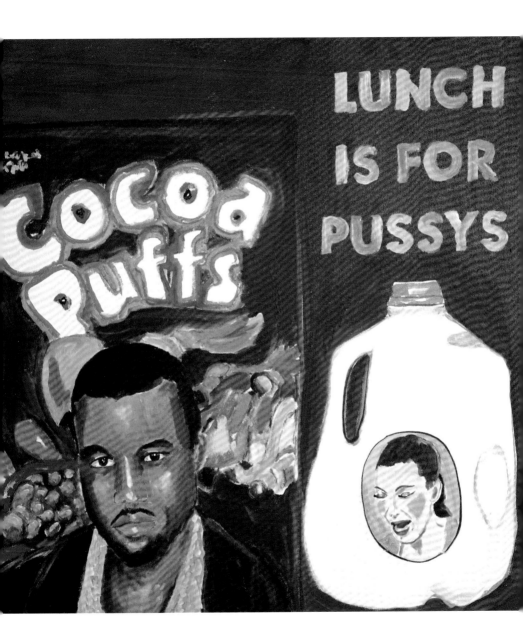

New Orleans and I have a tumultuous love affair. If I had to compare it to any type of couple, it would be an old Italian couple.

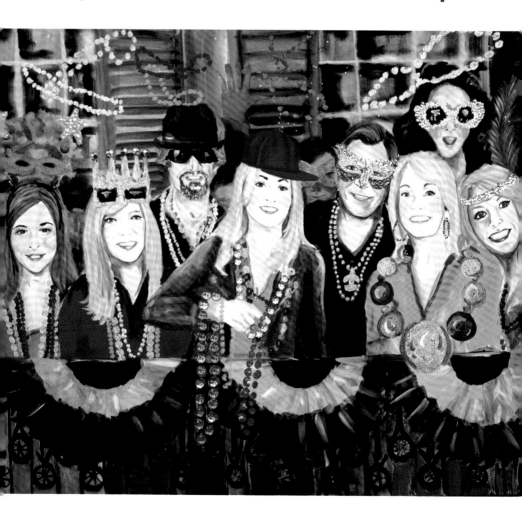

MEANING IN LIFE

Now that I've gotten older, I realize that life is all about the people you surround yourself with and the moments you share with them. There are moments when I'm with my friends or family, or even at work with my team, and they make me so happy I cry—and that's when I know I'm on the right path. And crying doesn't mean I'm hormonal, or crazy, or that I need a fucking Xanax and a drink. To have those feelings and be fully in that moment is the best feeling in the world.

NEW ORLEANS

New Orleans and I have a tumultuous love affair. If I had to compare it to any type of couple, it would be an old Italian couple. When I get upset, like when it's so fucking hot, or when the first ten minutes of the news is all about how many people have been murdered, I have my hands up in the air, and I'm yelling.

But what I love about this place is its rawness. If you do come to New Orleans, we're not trying to hide anything from you. We've got the good, the bad, and the fucking ugly all right here, and it makes one beautiful, fascinating beast. I love Mardi Gras, I love a second line band, I love a parade, I love drama, I love excess of every kind, and that is New Orleans. I love the courtyards and ivy-colored walls. There is a reason artists, musicians, and chefs flock to this place. It's bohemian and embraces all weirdness. It's the birthplace of jazz, for God's sake! People come to New Orleans to drink, eat, and listen to music. They want to be intoxicated by art, and everything else, for that matter.

NATURE

There's something intoxicating about oak trees covered in moss and the sound of cicadas at night. When I was little, I'd freak my friends out because I'd go collect bugs. In July, I would know when the luna moths would hatch, and I'd go watch their wings unfold. My friends thought it was disgusting, but I was fascinated by it. I always had jars with frogs, earthworms, and fireflies. That's something people never guess about me, but I love nature. In order for me to process this American greed, and this whirlwind I'm a part of, I need to go into the woods and give my brain a clean slate. It's like my very own (better) Garden Club.

YOU WANT TO BE HAPPY? GET OUT OF BED AND DO SOMETHING MEANINGFUL WITH YOUR LIFE.

PEGGY MCDOUGAL

She just popped out of my mouth in the George V Paris, straight from Wisconsin. Peggy is the ultimate Middle America woman. She's sexually repressed, she's dying to know life outside of the Cheesecake Factory, and she's gotten herself in financial trouble because they gave her a Target card and a Bed, Bath & Beyond card (she doesn't even care about the Bed & Bath—she only gives a shit about the Beyond). She's horny as fuck, loves to talk shit about her best friend, Patricia, wants to climb Bieber like a tree, and wants a rapper to do coke off her butthole.

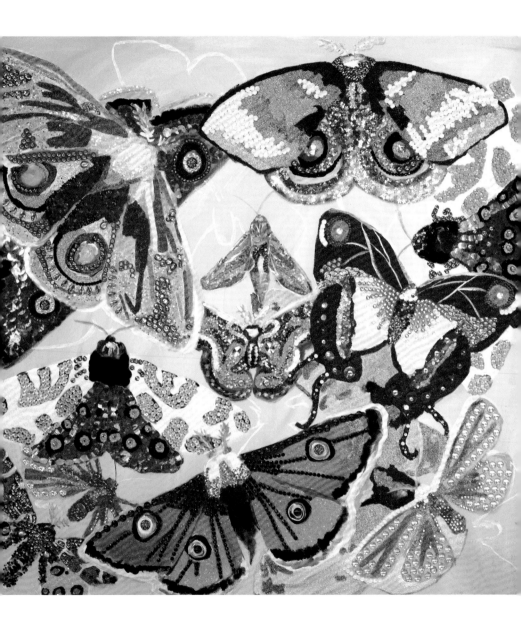

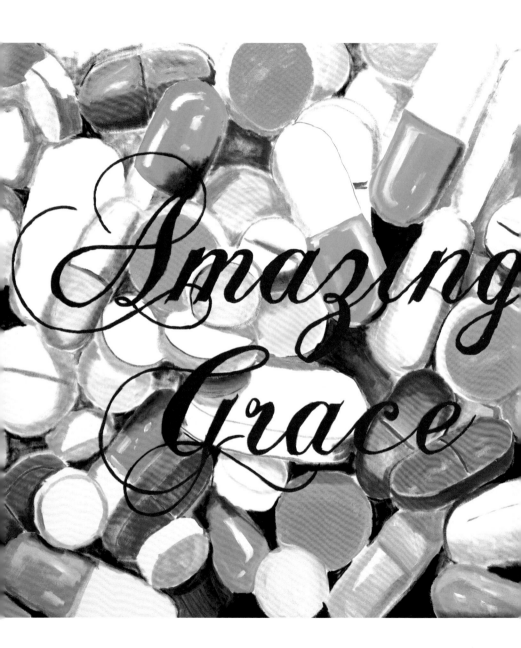

PENISES

Penises are fun, but I spend a lot of my time wondering how in the world men are just walking around with all that junk hanging between their legs. I'll be just sitting next to Michael, and I'll ask, "What is happening with your 'nads right now? Are they in between your thighs? Are they below them? How does that work?" It's not like titties, where I've got a bra and they're all pulled up (unless they're wearing a budgie-smuggler or banana hammock). Being an artist is a bit like being a scientist—we like to study shit. Sometimes our curiosity leads us to painting a giant penis or a pair of balls. It's only normal to be curious about something you don't have. Anyway, to me the penis is an awesome thing, but I'd take having a vagina any day. There's a reason that the female body is the most photographed thing on the planet.

PRESCRIPTION DRUGS

There's a pill for everything, and some of them actually work—they make your dick hard, they make that headache go away, they lower your cholesterol. But there's no happy pill, bitches. You want to be happy? Get out of bed and do something meaningful with your life.

I can hear self-medicated women coming from a mile away. I hear the little pill shakers in their purses when they come into the studio. They have prescriptions for Adderall so they don't eat all day, and Xanax to take them down when they have to pick the kids up from school. This attitude society has, that beauty is about being thin and taking pills, doesn't lead to happiness or health. We have to accept that we're not always going to be as skinny as we want to be and we're not always going to look as young as we want. Maybe if you're depressed, because you're hanging out with a bunch of cunts, the answer isn't taking a bunch of pills; the answer is not hanging out with those fucking cunts anymore. But, if they want to come into my studio, I'll give those ladies a glass of Champagne, and they can pop a Xanax, and I'll get all up in that Birkin bag.

POWER

You know what power is? Power isn't about stuff, or money, or status. Power is being able to take care of yourself. Physically, spiritually, emotionally, financially. That's the ultimate power, and there's nothing in the world like it. Power is not having to suck dick for anything.

SELF-LOVE

Now that I'm older, I wouldn't trade what I know now in my life and the confidence I have for perkier tits. In my twenties, I was a fiercely ambitchous and extremely goal-oriented girl, but I was very insecure about my body and myself. Now, I look back and think, *Jesus Christ, I looked pretty damn good back then.* All of my failures and experiences have made me brave. I really don't give a fuck. The only thing that is important is that I love me for me.

The beauty of me now is I can look at myself and I think: *Not only can I buy the things I want to buy, and create the things I want to create, and I contribute to society, but goddamn it, I love me some motherfucking me.* I like the way I look; I like the way my body is. Maybe if I were thinner, I wouldn't be as approachable. I'm a big fan of the self-loving, and not self-loathing. Your youth, your virginity, your reputation, they're all things you never know you have until they're fucking gone—so appreciate yourself and all you have.

Now that I'm older, I wouldn't trade what I know now in my life and the confidence I have for perkier tits.

POWER IS BEING ABLE TO TAKE CARE OF YOURSELF. PHYSICALLY, SPIRITUALLY, EMOTIONALLY, FINANCIALLY.

SEX AND RELATIONSHIPS

I love to watch the modern mating dance, especially now that I'm older. If you go somewhere like Miami, you'll see these young girls in thongs with their big fucking Kardashian asses, and they're bouncing around, trying to get the attention of men who are clearly renting Lamborghinis because they don't know the difference between turning on the blinker and turning on the windshield wipers. It's just all this big peacocking dance, and it's part of who we are as humans. I will say that I'm happy that I've found the love of my life, so I can focus my energy on being creative artistically, and not on being out on the town, cougaring around.

SHOPPING

Oh, I've had mad problems since I memorized my AmEx card number. I love nothing more than to turn down the AC to about 64, pile my dogs on my bed, yank out my laptop, and go to fucking town. I've got three companies now, and I don't have time to be shopping all day, so I love to online shop. This is a modern woman. This is how we do it . . . naked in the dark.

It's funny, I'll buy something and just hoard it for three or four months so it stays brand new, like new Gucci shoes or a kimono jacket. I covet them, I love them, and I can't believe they're mine. Sometimes I like to see how fast I can buy stuff online. I'll put my card information in, and I'll be like, *Oh, my god, I just spent fucking $15,000 in three minutes, then I go right ahead and check the return policy.*

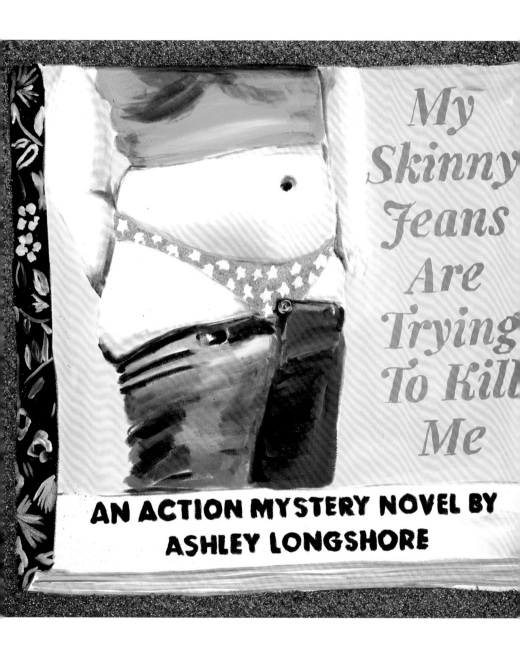

My
Skinny
Jeans
Are
Trying
To Kill
Me

**AN ACTION MYSTERY NOVEL BY
ASHLEY LONGSHORE**

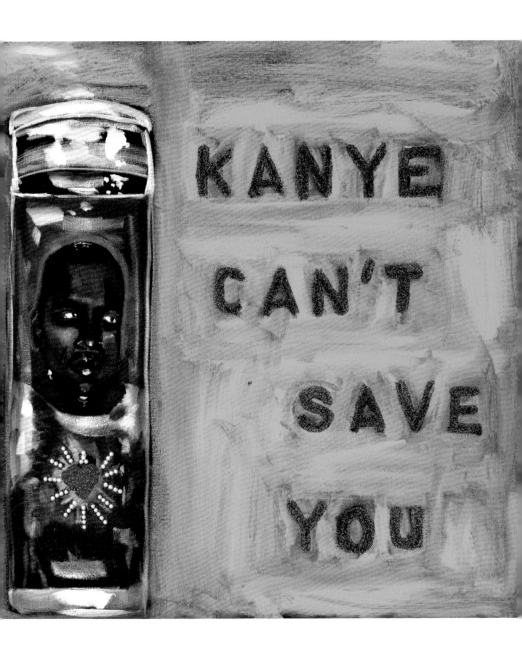

THE SOUTH

The South is a different dance; it's a different kind of bird. I think it's wonderful that manners are really important down here and that we still value formalities. It's an asset, and it's always been one to me, no matter where I go. People might see my social media and think I come in the room dropping f-bombs, but the opposite of that is true. I'm enthusiastic and gracious because the South raised me that way. The South—well, really my grandmother—taught me how, even when other people are being assholes, it's best to just bat your eyes and smile. And of course, when you can't bite your tongue, you can just drop the old "thank you so motherfucking much" on them and see how they react.

There are also parts of the South I don't love. The conservative up-bringing I had in Montgomery tried its hardest to mold me into another trophy wife, a follower. But luckily, that backfired and fueled the wonderful weirdness that has made me successful.

STRESS AND ANXIETY

Stress is the real deal. Everyone in this world feels it, and everyone has to deal with it in their own way. For me, if I'm sad or stressed, the only cure is action. My dad used to say, "They ain't gonna line up at the door. You ain't gonna get anywhere sitting around scratching your broke ass. You've got to get your fucking ass up and do something." If I'm feeling like I need to make some money, then I better paint a fucking painting. Once I've made that painting, I put it on Instagram, I make a video of it, and I send it to my top clients. Action, action, action, action. The only way to alleviate that anxiety is to knock shit off the fucking list. You can't just sit around, scratchin' around.

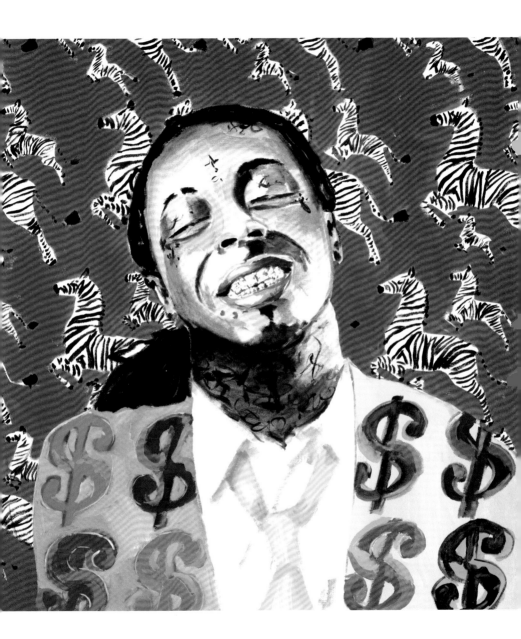

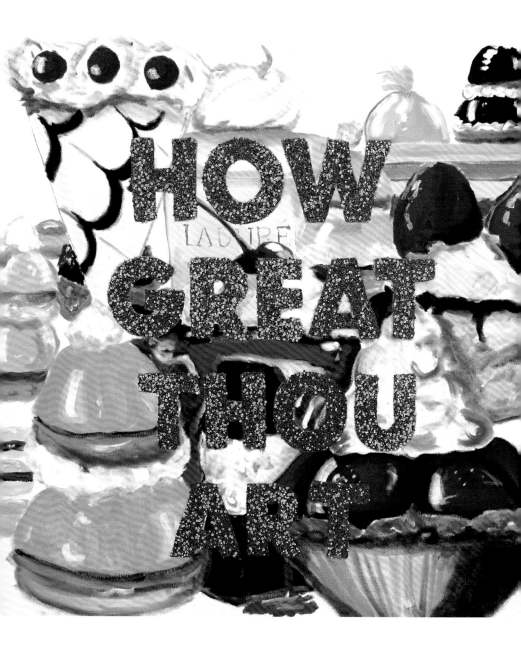

THINGS YOU EAT WHEN YOU EAT YOUR FEELINGS

As American women, we've been taught that we have to be a million things: We have to be thin, rich, live on the right street, be successful—but not too successful—and if you have kids, they have to be straight out of a Rockwell painting. It's just too much goddamn pressure, and sometimes nothing can make that hate go away like a slice of pecan pie. For me, I like pizza, and if I were going to get electrocuted tomorrow, my last supper would be chicken strips and ice cream.

"THIS IS A STICKUP"

A mystery novel about pussy stuff. This painting is about the new woman. A woman who has power. This doesn't mean she hates men, and it doesn't mean she hates other women. She is embracing all the positive things about herself and using that energy to be a bad mother-fucking bitch.

VAGINAS

GIVE ME A V!!! I feel so lucky to have a pussy. They're fun, they're funny, and they're fucking crazy. A vagina is a mysterious fucking thing; it's a bit like Pandora's box. I like to think that maybe the vagina is this massive antenna for all that is happening in the universe. Maybe it's where we women get our intuition. Women are amazing creatures; we have this extra thing that allows us to be the mother, the wife, the lover, the businessperson, the multitasker—all at the same time. To have a pussy is the most awesome fucking thing on the planet.

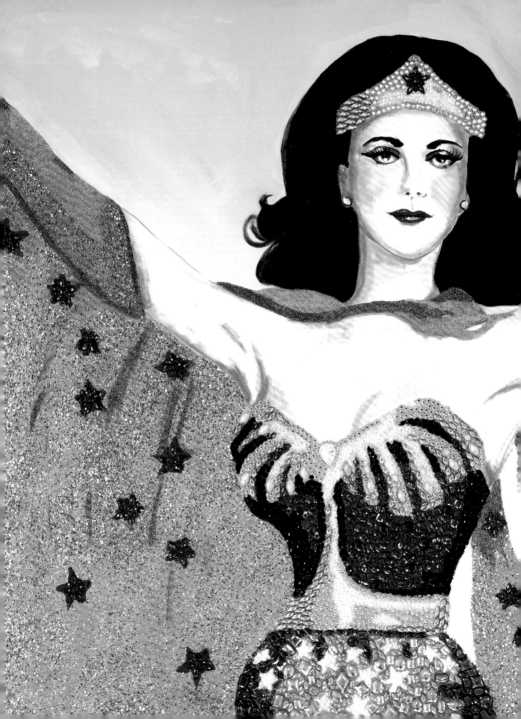

You will make your own dinner and you will love it.

WHO'S RUNNING THINGS? WELL, YOU ARE, WONDER WOMAN.

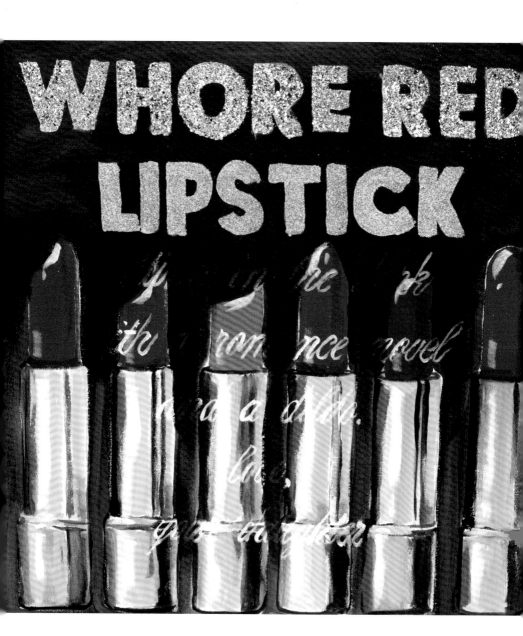

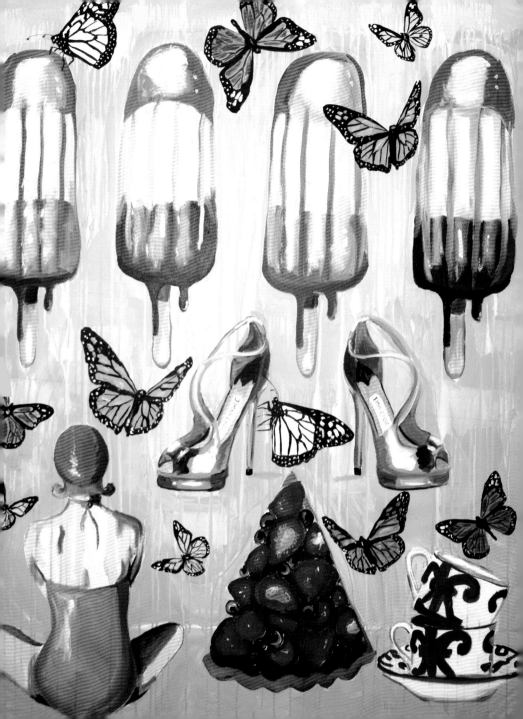

"WHORE RED LIPSTICK"

This one's for my mother. Every time she saw a woman with red lipstick, she'd turn to me and say, "Look at that whore in that whore-red lipstick." And now, thanks to her, whore red is my favorite lipstick color.

"WONDER WOMAN"

If you're a Woman who truly embraces every opportunity, who faces the world head on, your power is unlimited. That's what this painting means. Who's running things? Well, you are, Wonder Woman.

"YOU DIDN'T GO TO HARVARD AND YOU AIN'T FAMOUS—NOW WHAT?"

This country is all about branding, your pedigree, and what street your house is on. If you say you went to Harvard, people are immediately like "Ooh, you must be amazing." If you didn't go to Harvard, and you ain't famous, you're either going to be sucking for it or working for it. They're both jobs—one of them just happens to be the oldest job in the goddamn world.

Yale

UNIVERSITY PRESS

Ashley Longshore

YOU DIDN'T GO TO HARVARD AND YOU AIN'T FAMOUS... NOW WHAT?

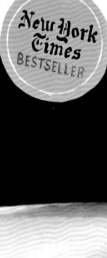

New York Times BESTSELLER

Acknowledgments

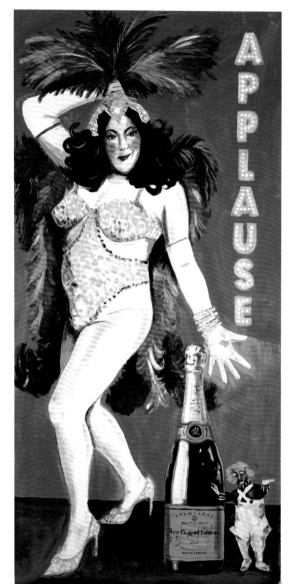

MY TEAM! Kate Grace Bauer, my amazing gallery director, Rachel Brown, Shannon Thomas, Sofia Ricardo, Jessy Fofana! My Sicilian grandfather Ernest Lupinacci who found me on Instagram and was the spark who made this wildness happen. To the incredible Judith Regan who is a trail blazer for women and is absolutely SUPERPUSSY.

My florist Monique Chauvin who keeps me surrounded by orchids. Nikki Epstein, who keeps my garden gorgeous and keeps flowers blooming all around me. I'd like to thank the great city of New Orleans for giving me the most fertile wild soil to be creative in. This city inspires all of my wildness and confidence. My best friends who have stuck by my wild, dramatic ass for life, and in memory of Patrick B Hale, my sweet friend who I know is with me every second.

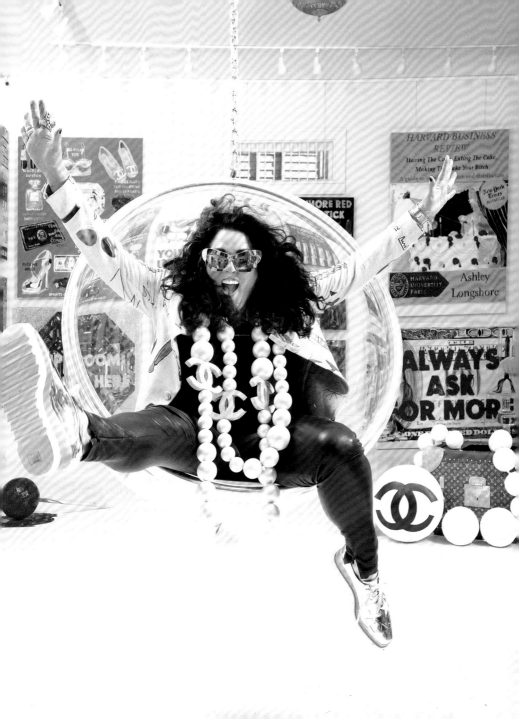

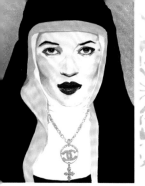
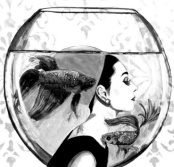
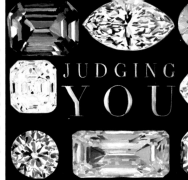
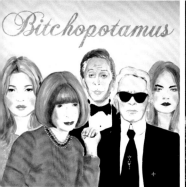
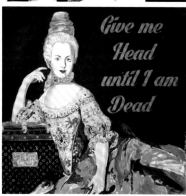
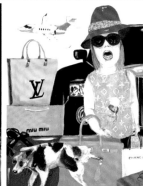

About the Artiste /
Superpussy / Author

ASHLEY LONGSHORE'S pop art paintings are never shy of daring. A prolific artist at a pivotal moment in her career, Ashley has been compared to Andy Warhol for her obsession with pop culture figures and brands as well as her relationships with celebrities. She has had major collaborations with brands such as Clé de Peau and Anthropologie and has emblazoned the path for pop art and fashion to coexist. Her work has been featured in magazines in both the United States and countries around the world including Switzerland, Belgium, Japan, and Australia, where collectors have begun to acquire her unique pieces. Her celebrity clientele includes Blake Lively, who describes Ashley's work as "elegant yet rebellious." She lives in New Orleans, home to the Ashley Longshore Studio Gallery.